The Food Kitchen Lab Cookbook with Scientific Techniques:

Unlocking Culinary Excellence at Home

CONTENTS

INTRODUCTION 8

PART 1: FUNDAMENTALS OF COOKING 18

    KITCHEN BASICS 19

    COOKING TECHNIQUES 31

PART 2: BREAKFAST AND BRUNCH 53

    1) Perfect Scrambled Eggs 54

    2) Fluffy Omelet 56

    3) Classic Pancakes and Waffles 58

    4) Homemade Bread and Rolls 63

    5) Savory and Sweet Pastries 66

    6) Fresh Juices and Smoothies 70

    7) Coffee and Tea Variations 73

PART 3: APPETIZERS AND SNACKS 77

    8) Vegetable Samosas 78

    9) Meatballs 82

    10) Dips and Spreads: Hummus and Baba Ganoush 86

11) Fresh Garden Salads 89

12) Hearty Lentil Soup 93

13) Chilled Gazpacho 96

PART 4: MAIN COURSES 100

14) Perfectly Roasted Chicken 101

15) Chicken Curry 104

16) Grilled Chicken Kebabs 107

17) Pan-Fried Steaks 110

18) Slow-Cooked Beef Stew 113

19) Lamb Tagine 117

20) Grilled Fish Fillets 121

21) Shrimp Stir-Fry 123

22) Baked Salmon 127

23) Stuffed Bell Peppers 130

24) Chickpea and Spinach Curry 133

25) Grilled Vegetable Platter 138

PART 5: SIDE DISHES 141

26) Roasted Root Vegetables 142

- 27) Grilled Asparagus 147
- 28) Perfectly Cooked Rice 150
- 29) Quinoa Salad 153
- 30) Homemade Pasta 161
- 31) Classic Spaghetti with Tomato Sauce 164
- 32) Stir-Fried Noodles 167

PART 6: DESSERTS 172

- 33) Classic Chocolate Cake 173
- 34) Biscotti 177
- 35) Traditional Baklava 180
- 36) Lemon Tart 184
- 37) Classic Apple Pie 189
- 38) Mini Fruit Tarts 194
- 39) Creamy Rice Pudding 198
- 40) Crème Brûlée 202
- 41) Chocolate Mousse 205

PART 7: SPECIAL OCCASIONS 209

- 42) Beef and Vegetable Stew 212

43) Macaroni and Cheese 214

44) Buffalo Chicken Dip 216

45) Caprese Salad Skewers 218

46) Mini Pizza Bites 219

47) Chicken and Vegetable Skewers 220

48) Veggie Quesadillas 221

49) Banana Oatmeal Cookies 222

50) Herb-Crusted Rack of Lamb 224

51) Lobster Risotto 225

52) Chocolate Soufflé 227

53) Grilled BBQ Chicken Drumsticks 229

54) Grilled Corn on the Cob with Herb Butter . 230

55) Grilled Veggie Skewers 231

56) Grilled Pineapple with Honey and Cinnamon 232

57) Cucumber and Cream Cheese Sandwiches: 233

58) Smoked Salmon and Dill Sandwiches: 234

59) Classic Scones with Clotted Cream and Jam 235

60) Mini Lemon Tarts:..236

APPENDICES..239

GOLOSARY OF TERMS..239

REFERENCES...250

INTRODUCTION

Welcome to "The Food Lab cooking for better life: Science based cooking for home safety." This book explores the intersection of culinary artistry and scientific understanding, offering readers a comprehensive guide to mastering the kitchen. From understanding the fundamentals of cooking techniques to discovering essential kitchen tools and ingredients, this book aims to empower both novice and seasoned cooks with the knowledge to create delicious and safe meals at home.

Cooking is more than just preparing food; it is a blend of art and science. Understanding the principles behind cooking techniques can elevate your dishes from ordinary to extraordinary. In "The Food Lab," we delve into the science behind cooking, exploring how different ingredients and methods interact to create mouthwatering flavors and textures. By understanding these scientific principles, you will gain the confidence to experiment in the kitchen and create dishes that are not only delicious but also consistent and reliable.

One of the unique aspects of this book is its focus on halal cooking. Halal, which means permissible in Arabic, is a dietary standard observed by millions of people around the world. In addition to providing a wide range of recipes that adhere to halal guidelines, we will explore the principles behind halal cooking, helping you to understand the importance of ingredient selection and preparation methods in maintaining dietary compliance.

"The Food Lab" is organized into several sections, each focusing on a different aspect of cooking. We start with the fundamentals, covering essential kitchen tools and ingredients, and move on to explore various cooking techniques, seasoning and flavoring, and specific meal categories such as breakfast, appetizers, main courses, side dishes, and desserts. Each chapter is designed to build your skills and knowledge, providing you with a comprehensive understanding of the culinary arts.

In addition to recipes and techniques, "The Food Lab" also addresses the importance of food safety. We provide guidelines on how to handle ingredients properly, maintain cleanliness in the kitchen, and ensure that your meals are safe to eat. By following these guidelines, you can protect yourself and your loved ones from foodborne illnesses and enjoy your meals with peace of mind.

We believe that cooking should be a joyous and fulfilling experience. With "The Food Lab," we aim to make your time in the kitchen enjoyable, educational, and rewarding. So, whether you are preparing a simple weeknight dinner or an elaborate feast for a special occasion, let this book be your trusted companion. Welcome to "The Food Lab," where cooking meets science for a better, safer, and more delicious life.

The Science of Cooking

Cooking is a remarkable blend of art and science, where understanding the underlying scientific principles can significantly enhance your culinary skills. The science of cooking delves into the interactions between heat, energy, and molecules, transforming raw ingredients into delectable dishes. This chapter will explore the fundamental scientific concepts that every home cook should know, providing a solid foundation for mastering various cooking techniques and achieving consistent, delicious results.

At its core, cooking is about applying heat to food. The way heat is transferred to food—through conduction, convection, or radiation—affects the texture, flavor, and overall quality of the dish. Conduction occurs when heat is transferred directly from a hot surface to the food, such as when searing a steak in a hot pan. Convection involves the movement of hot air or liquid around the food, as seen in roasting or boiling. Radiation, on the other hand, transfers heat through electromagnetic waves, like grilling or broiling.

Temperature plays a crucial role in cooking. Different cooking methods require specific temperature ranges to achieve desired results. For instance, low and slow cooking methods, such as braising and stewing, break down tough connective tissues in meat, resulting in tender and flavorful dishes. High-temperature methods, like grilling and frying, create Maillard reactions, where amino acids and reducing sugars interact to form complex flavors and a desirable brown crust.

The Maillard reaction, named after French chemist Louis-Camille Maillard, is a cornerstone of the science of cooking. This reaction occurs between amino acids and reducing sugars at temperatures above 300°F (150°C) and is responsible for the browning of meat, the toasty flavor of bread crust, and the rich color of roasted coffee. Understanding how to control the Maillard reaction can help you achieve perfect sears on meats, beautifully caramelized vegetables, and deeply flavored sauces.

Another essential scientific concept in cooking is the role of water. Water is a versatile medium in cooking, involved in boiling, steaming, braising, and more. The way water interacts with food affects its texture and moisture content. For example, steaming preserves the natural moisture and nutrients of vegetables, while boiling can lead to nutrient loss if not done properly. The gelatinization of starches in water is also key to making sauces and gravies, where starch granules absorb water, swell, and thicken the liquid.

Emulsification is another fascinating scientific phenomenon in cooking. An emulsion is a mixture of two immiscible liquids, such as oil and water, stabilized by an emulsifier. Common emulsifiers include egg yolks in mayonnaise, mustard in vinaigrettes, and lecithin in chocolate. Understanding emulsification can help you create stable, creamy dressings, sauces, and even ice creams.

PH levels also influence cooking outcomes. The acidity or alkalinity of ingredients affects their texture, flavor, and color. For instance, adding an acidic ingredient like vinegar or lemon juice to a marinade can tenderize meat by breaking down proteins. Baking soda, an alkaline substance, helps baked goods rise by producing carbon dioxide gas when it reacts with an acid. Balancing pH levels is crucial in cooking processes like making jam, where the right acidity ensures proper gelling and preservation.

In "The Food Lab," we will explore these scientific principles and more, providing you with the knowledge to understand and control the cooking process. By mastering the science of cooking, you can elevate your culinary creations, achieving consistent, delicious results every time. So, embrace the science, experiment with techniques, and let your kitchen become a laboratory of flavors and textures. Welcome to the fascinating world of the science of cooking.

Essential Kitchen Tools and Ingredients

A well-equipped kitchen is the cornerstone of successful cooking. Having the right tools and ingredients at your disposal not only makes the cooking process more efficient but also enhances the quality of your dishes. In this chapter, we will explore the essential kitchen tools and ingredients that every home cook should have, ensuring you are well-prepared to tackle any recipe with confidence.

Essential Kitchen Tools

1. **Chef's Knife** a high-quality chef's knife is indispensable in any kitchen. It is versatile, capable of handling a variety of tasks from chopping vegetables to slicing meat. Invest in a knife that feels comfortable in your hand and maintains a sharp edge.

2. **Cutting Board** A sturdy cutting board is essential for safe and efficient food preparation. Wooden or bamboo cutting boards are gentle on knives, while plastic boards are easy to sanitize. Having multiple boards to separate raw meat from vegetables is a good practice for preventing cross-contamination.

3. **Measuring Cups and Spoons** Accurate measurements are crucial in cooking, especially in baking. A set of measuring cups and spoons ensures you add the right amount of ingredients, leading to consistent and reliable results.

4. **Mixing Bowls** A variety of mixing bowls in different sizes is useful for preparing ingredients, mixing batters, and tossing salads. Stainless steel, glass, and plastic bowls each have their

own advantages, so choose based on your preference and needs.

5. **Skillets and Saucepans** Quality skillets and saucepans are essential for various cooking methods, from sautéing and frying to simmering and boiling. Non-stick skillets are great for delicate foods like eggs, while stainless steel or cast-iron pans provide excellent heat retention and searing capabilities.

6. **Baking Sheets and Pans** Baking sheets and pans are necessary for baking cookies, roasting vegetables, and cooking sheet-pan meals. Opt for heavy-duty, warp-resistant options to ensure even cooking and durability.

7. **Wooden Spoons and Spatulas** Wooden spoons and spatulas are gentle on cookware surfaces and ideal for stirring, mixing, and scraping. They are heat-resistant and won't scratch non-stick pans.

8. **Whisk** A whisk is essential for beating eggs, blending sauces, and mixing dry ingredients. A balloon whisk is versatile and works well for most tasks, while a flat whisk is great for making gravies and sauces.

9. **Tongs** Tongs are perfect for flipping meats, tossing salads, and serving hot dishes. Look for

tongs with a comfortable grip and a locking mechanism for easy storage.

10. **Microplane Grater** A microplane grater is excellent for zesting citrus, grating cheese, and finely mincing garlic or ginger. Its sharp blades make quick work of these tasks, enhancing the flavors in your dishes.

Essential Ingredients

1. **Salt** Salt is the most fundamental seasoning in cooking. It enhances flavors, balances sweetness, and can even affect the texture of certain dishes. Keep both fine table salt and coarse kosher or sea salt on hand for different applications.

2. **Pepper** Freshly ground black pepper adds a robust flavor to dishes. Invest in a good pepper mill and whole peppercorns to ensure the freshest taste.

3. **Olive Oil** Olive oil is a versatile cooking fat, perfect for sautéing, roasting, and making dressings. Extra virgin olive oil offers the best flavor for salads and finishing dishes, while regular olive oil is suitable for cooking.

4. **Vinegars** Vinegars add acidity and brightness to dishes. Apple cider vinegar, balsamic vinegar, and vinegar are all versatile options that can be used in marinades, dressings, and sauces.

5. **Herbs and Spices** a well-stocked spice rack is essential for adding depth and complexity to your cooking. Common spices include cumin, paprika, turmeric, and cinnamon, while fresh herbs like parsley, cilantro, and basil bring vibrant flavors to your dishes.

6. **Garlic and Onions** Garlic and onions form the base of countless recipes, providing a savory foundation that enhances other flavors. Keep fresh garlic cloves and a variety of onions, such as yellow, red, and shallots, in your pantry.

7. **Flour** All-purpose flour is a versatile ingredient used in baking, thickening sauces, and coating foods for frying. Store it in an airtight container to keep it fresh.

8. **Sugar** Granulated sugar, brown sugar, and confectioners' sugar are all useful for baking and cooking. Each type of sugar has its own unique properties and flavor contributions.

9. **Canned Tomatoes** Canned tomatoes are a convenient and flavorful ingredient for sauces, stews, and soups. Keep whole, diced, and crushed tomatoes in your pantry for various recipes.

10. **Broth or Stock** Chicken, beef, and vegetable broth or stock add depth to soups, stews, and

sauces. Homemade or store-bought, they are essential for building flavor in many dishes.

By equipping your kitchen with these essential tools and ingredients, you will be ready to tackle a wide range of recipes with confidence. Understanding how to use these tools and ingredients effectively will not only make your cooking more efficient but also elevate the taste and quality of your dishes. So, gather your tools, stock your pantry, and get ready to embark on a delicious culinary journey with "The Food Lab."

PART 1: FUNDAMENTALS OF COOKING

In this foundational section, we delve into the essentials that form the backbone of culinary expertise. From mastering basic kitchen skills and techniques to understanding how heat affects food, you'll build a solid understanding of the principles that govern cooking. Whether you're learning to bake, roast, grill, or experiment with braising and stewing, these techniques will set the stage for culinary success.

KITCHEN BASICS

Understanding Ingredients

Ingredients are the building blocks of cooking. Knowing how to select, handle, and combine them is crucial for creating delicious and nutritious meals. This chapter will guide you through the fundamentals of understanding ingredients, focusing on their characteristics, roles in recipes, and how to make the best choices for your culinary creations.

The Role of Ingredients

Each ingredient in a recipe has a specific role to play, whether it's providing structure, flavor, moisture, or color. Understanding these roles helps you make informed decisions when shopping for, substituting, or modifying ingredients.

1. **Proteins**:
    - **Meat and Poultry**: These are rich sources of protein and flavor. Different cuts have varying textures and cooking requirements. For example, tender cuts like chicken breast and beef tenderloin are best cooked quickly using dry heat methods, while tougher cuts like beef chuck and lamb shoulder benefit from slow, moist cooking methods.

- **Seafood**: Fish and shellfish are versatile and cook quickly. Freshness is key, so look for clear eyes, firm flesh, and a clean smell.

- **Plant-Based Proteins**: Beans, lentils, tofu, and tempeh are excellent sources of protein for vegetarian and vegan diets. They offer different textures and flavors and can be used in a variety of dishes.

2. **Fruits and Vegetables**:

    - **Freshness and Seasonality**: Choose fruits and vegetables that are in season for the best flavor and nutritional value. Local produce is often fresher and more environmentally friendly.

    - **Preparation**: Different cooking methods bring out different qualities in vegetables. Roasting enhances sweetness, while steaming preserves nutrients and color. Fruits can be enjoyed fresh, or cooked to create sauces, desserts, and compotes.

3. **Grains and Starches**:

    - **Varieties**: There are many types of grains and starches, including rice, quinoa, barley, pasta, and potatoes. Each has unique cooking requirements and nutritional profiles.

- **Cooking Techniques**: Grains generally need to be cooked in water or broth. Understanding the correct water-to-grain ratio and cooking time is essential for achieving the desired texture.

4. **Dairy and Alternatives**:

    - **Dairy**: Milk, cheese, butter, and yogurt are staple ingredients that add richness, flavor, and texture to dishes. They also play critical roles in baking and dessert making.

    - **Non-Dairy Alternatives**: Plant-based milks, cheeses, and yogurts are suitable for those who are lactose intolerant or following a vegan diet. They vary in flavor and performance, so choose based on the specific needs of your recipe.

5. **Fats and Oils**:

    - **Types of Fats**: Butter, olive oil, coconut oil, and vegetable oil are common fats used in cooking. Each has a different smoke point and flavor profile, affecting how and when they should be used.

- **Health Considerations**: While fats are essential for flavor and texture, it's important to use them in moderation and choose healthier options when possible.

6. **Seasonings and Aromatics**:
   - **Herbs and Spices**: These are critical for adding flavor and complexity to dishes. Fresh herbs like basil and cilantro are best added at the end of cooking, while dried spices like cumin and paprika benefit from being added early to allow their flavors to develop.
   - **Aromatics**: Ingredients like garlic, onions, ginger, and leeks form the base of many recipes, providing a depth of flavor that builds as they cook.

Selecting Quality Ingredients

Choosing the best quality ingredients is vital for achieving the best results in your cooking. Here are some tips for selecting various types of ingredients:

1. **Meat and Poultry**: Look for meat that is bright in color, with a firm texture and little to no odor. For poultry, check for clear skin and avoid any with a slimy texture or off smell.

2. **Seafood**: Fresh seafood should smell like the ocean, not fishy. Shellfish should be tightly closed, and fillets should be firm and glistening.

3. **Produce**: Select fruits and vegetables that are vibrant in color, firm to the touch, and free of blemishes or soft spots. For leafy greens, avoid any with yellowing or wilting leaves.

4. **Grains and Legumes**: Ensure they are dry, clean, and free from any signs of pests or mold. Store them in airtight containers to maintain freshness.

5. **Dairy**: Check the expiration dates and look for products with the least amount of added ingredients. Fresh dairy should have a clean smell and a consistent texture.

6. **Fats and Oils**: Choose oils that are cold-pressed and minimally processed. Store them in a cool, dark place to prevent rancidity.

Ingredient Substitutions

Understanding how to substitute ingredients can be a lifesaver in the kitchen. Here are some common substitutions:

1. **Butter**: Can be substituted with margarine or oil in most recipes. For baking, applesauce or mashed bananas can replace some or all of the butter for a lower-fat option.

2. **Eggs**: In baking, eggs can be substituted with flaxseed meal (1 tablespoon flaxseed meal + 3 tablespoons water = 1 egg), applesauce, or commercial egg replacers.

3. **Milk**: Non-dairy milks like almond, soy, or oat milk can replace cow's milk in most recipes. Choose unsweetened versions to control the flavor.

4. **Sugar**: Honey, maple syrup, or agave nectar can replace sugar, though you may need to adjust the liquid content of the recipe. Stevia and other non-caloric sweeteners are also options.

5. **Flour**: Gluten-free flours like almond flour, coconut flour, or a commercial gluten-free blend can replace all-purpose flour in most recipes, though the texture may differ.

By understanding the characteristics and roles of ingredients, you can make informed choices that enhance your cooking. This knowledge allows you to adapt recipes, experiment with new flavors, and create dishes that are both delicious and nutritionally balanced. So, embrace the diversity of ingredients available and let your culinary creativity flourish.

Knife Skills and Techniques

Mastering knife skills is fundamental to efficient and enjoyable cooking. Proper knife techniques not only enhance safety but also improve the precision and presentation of your dishes. This chapter will guide you through essential knife skills and techniques, helping you to handle your knives with confidence and expertise.

Choosing the Right Knife

1. **Chef's Knife**:
    - The most versatile knife in the kitchen, ideal for chopping, slicing, dicing, and mincing. It typically has an 8 to 10-inch blade.

2. **Paring Knife**:
    - A small knife with a 3 to 4-inch blade, perfect for intricate tasks such as peeling, trimming, and detailed cutting.

3. **Serrated Knife**:
    - With a saw-like edge, this knife is excellent for cutting through bread, tomatoes, and other foods with tough exteriors and soft interiors.

4. **Boning Knife**:
    - A narrow, flexible blade designed for deboning meat and fish.

Knife Safety

1. **Grip**:
    - Hold the knife with a firm grip, wrapping your fingers around the handle. Your thumb and index finger should grasp the blade just in front of the handle for better control.

2. **Cutting Technique**:
    - Use a rocking motion, keeping the tip of the knife on the cutting board and moving the blade in an arc. This technique is efficient and reduces strain on your wrist.

3. **Cutting Surface**:
    - Always use a stable, non-slip cutting board. Place a damp cloth or paper towel under the board to prevent it from moving.

4. **Knife Maintenance**:
    - Keep your knives sharp using a honing rod regularly and sharpen them with a whetstone or professional service as needed. A sharp knife is safer than a dull one because it requires less force to cut through food.

Basic Knife Cuts

1. **Chopping**:
    - For larger, rough cuts. Place the food on the cutting board, stabilize it with your non-dominant hand (using a claw grip to protect your fingers), and chop with a quick downward motion.

2. **Dicing**:
    - For uniform, smaller cubes. First, slice the food into even strips, then cut the strips crosswise into cubes. Commonly used for vegetables like onions, carrots, and bell peppers.

3. **Slicing**:
    - For even, thin pieces. Use a smooth, continuous motion to cut through the food. Ideal for meats, fish, and vegetables.

4. **Julienning**:
    - For matchstick-sized pieces. Slice the food into thin planks, then stack and cut them into even strips. This technique is perfect for stir-fries and garnishes.

5. **Mincing**:

- For very fine, tiny pieces. Often used for garlic, ginger, and herbs. Start by finely chopping, then continue to cut with a rocking motion until the desired fineness is achieved.

Advanced Knife Techniques

1. **Chiffonade**:
   - For cutting leafy greens and herbs into thin ribbons. Stack the leaves, roll them tightly, and then slice crosswise. Commonly used for basil and spinach.

2. **Butterflying**:
   - For creating a thinner, more even piece of meat. Slice horizontally through the thickest part of the meat, stopping just before cutting all the way through, then open it like a book.

3. **Supreming**:
   - For segmenting citrus fruits. Cut off the top and bottom, then slice away the peel and pith. Use a paring knife to cut between the membranes, releasing the segments.

Knife Care and Maintenance

1. **Cleaning**:
   - Hand wash knives immediately after use with mild soap and water. Dry them thoroughly to prevent rust and corrosion. Avoid putting knives in the dishwasher, as the harsh detergents and high heat can damage the blade and handle.

2. **Storage**:
   - Store knives in a knife block, magnetic strip, or knife guard to protect the blades and prevent accidents. Avoid storing knives loosely in a drawer.

3. **Sharpening and Honing**:
   - Hone your knife regularly with a honing rod to maintain its edge. Sharpen your knife with a whetstone or have it professionally sharpened to restore the blade's sharpness.

Practicing Knife Skills

1. **Start Slow**:
   - Practice basic cuts slowly and deliberately, focusing on consistency and control. Speed will come with practice.

2. **Practice on Different Foods**:

- Different ingredients require different techniques. Practice on a variety of foods to develop a well-rounded skill set.

3. **Mind Your Fingers**:
    - Always use the claw grip, curling your fingers under and keeping them away from the blade.

4. **Watch Tutorials**:
    - Online tutorials and cooking classes can provide visual guidance and tips from professionals.

Mastering knife skills is a journey that requires patience and practice. With these techniques and tips, you'll become more efficient in the kitchen, enhance the presentation of your dishes, and most importantly, ensure your safety. So grab your knife, start practicing, and enjoy the process of becoming a skilled and confident cook.

COOKING TECHNIQUES

Heat and Its Effects on Food

Heat is a fundamental element in cooking, transforming raw ingredients into delicious and safe-to-eat dishes. Understanding how heat affects food at a molecular level can significantly improve your cooking skills. There are three primary methods of heat transfer: conduction, convection, and radiation, each interacting with food in unique ways to create a variety of textures, flavors, and nutritional profiles.

Conduction is the process of heat transferring from one molecule to another through direct contact. This method is prevalent in cooking techniques such as sautéing and pan-frying, where food is placed on a hot surface like a skillet or grill. As the heat travels from the surface to the food, it causes the proteins to denature and coagulate, the carbohydrates to caramelize, and the fats to melt. These changes result in the Maillard reaction, a chemical reaction between amino acids and reducing sugars that gives browned foods their distinctive flavor and color. The Maillard reaction is responsible for the savory crust on a steak, the golden hue of toasted bread, and the rich flavors of roasted coffee.

Convection involves the transfer of heat through a fluid medium, such as air or water. This method is utilized in baking, roasting, boiling, and steaming. In convection cooking, the hot air or liquid circulates around the food, cooking it evenly. The circulating heat not only cooks food more uniformly but also speeds up the cooking process. For example, roasting a chicken in a convection oven results in a crisp, evenly browned skin while keeping the meat juicy and tender. Similarly, boiling vegetables in water or steaming them allows for even heat distribution, preserving their color, texture, and nutrients.

Radiation, the third method, transfers heat through electromagnetic waves. This is observed in cooking techniques such as grilling, broiling, and microwaving. When food is exposed to radiant heat, energy is absorbed by its molecules, causing them to vibrate and generate heat internally. Grilling a piece of fish, for instance, exposes it to intense radiant heat from the grill's flames, quickly cooking the exterior while maintaining a moist and flaky interior. Microwaving, on the other hand, uses microwave radiation to agitate water molecules within the food, generating heat and cooking it from the inside out. This method is particularly efficient for reheating and cooking small portions quickly.

Heat also plays a critical role in food safety by killing harmful bacteria and pathogens. Cooking meat to the appropriate internal temperature ensures that it is safe to eat, while pasteurizing milk and other dairy products eliminates harmful microorganisms without compromising their nutritional value. Moreover, heat enhances the digestibility and bioavailability of nutrients. Cooking vegetables, for instance, breaks down their tough cell walls, making it easier for our bodies to absorb their vitamins and minerals. However, it is important to balance cooking methods and times, as excessive heat can degrade certain nutrients, such as vitamin C and some B vitamins.

Understanding the effects of heat on food allows cooks to manipulate textures and flavors creatively. Slow cooking methods like braising and stewing break down tough connective tissues in meat, resulting in tender, flavorful dishes. Quick, high-heat methods like stir-frying preserve the vibrant colors and crisp textures of vegetables while developing rich, savory flavors. By mastering the principles of heat transfer and its effects on food, you can elevate your cooking techniques, create more flavorful dishes, and ensure food safety and nutrition. Whether you're searing a steak to perfection, baking a batch of cookies, or steaming a medley of vegetables, harnessing the power of heat is essential to culinary success.

Dry Heat Cooking Methods: Baking, Roasting, Grilling

Dry heat cooking methods, which include baking, roasting, and grilling, use air or direct heat to cook food, creating complex flavors and appealing textures without the need for added moisture. These techniques are staples in the culinary world, each offering distinct advantages and effects on food.

Baking

Baking is a versatile cooking method that uses dry heat in an enclosed space, typically an oven. This technique is commonly used for a wide range of foods, from bread and pastries to casseroles and vegetables. The steady, even heat of the oven allows for precise control over the cooking process. When baking, the heat causes the food's surface to brown and caramelize, developing rich flavors and a pleasant texture. The interior of baked goods, like cakes and bread, undergoes a chemical transformation as leavening agents such as yeast, baking powder, or baking soda create gas bubbles, causing the dough or batter to rise. This results in a light, airy structure in bread and cakes, while pastries achieve a flaky, tender consistency.

Roasting

Roasting is similar to baking but typically refers to cooking meat, poultry, and vegetables at higher temperatures. This method is renowned for its ability to create a crisp, caramelized exterior while keeping the interior moist and flavorful. Roasting is performed in an open, dry environment, often on a rack to allow heat to circulate evenly around the food. For meats, the high heat initially sears the surface, locking in juices and developing a savory crust through the Maillard reaction. As the food continues to cook, the heat penetrates the interior, breaking down connective tissues and rendering fats, resulting in tender, succulent dishes. Vegetables roasted at high temperatures caramelize, concentrating their natural sugars and enhancing their flavors, which is why roasted root vegetables or Brussels sprouts often taste sweeter and more complex than their raw counterparts.

Grilling

Grilling involves cooking food over an open flame or hot coals, imparting a distinctive smoky flavor and appealing grill marks. This high-heat method is ideal for quick-cooking proteins such as steaks, burgers, chicken breasts, and fish, as well as vegetables like bell peppers, zucchini, and corn. Grilling cooks food rapidly, with the direct heat from the flame or coals searing the surface and creating a flavorful crust. The intense heat also caramelizes the sugars in marinades and sauces, adding depth and complexity to the dish. To grill successfully, it's essential to preheat the grill to the appropriate temperature, oil the grates to prevent sticking, and monitor the food closely to avoid overcooking or burning. Grilling not only enhances the taste and texture of food but also creates a visually appealing presentation, making it a favorite method for outdoor cooking and social gatherings.

Benefits and Considerations

Dry heat cooking methods offer numerous benefits. They typically require less added fat, making them a healthier option for many dishes. The high temperatures and direct heat enhance the natural flavors of food, reduce cooking times, and create desirable textures. However, these methods also require careful attention to avoid overcooking or burning, which can lead to a loss of nutrients and unpleasant flavors. Additionally, the Maillard reaction and caramelization, while delicious, can produce potentially harmful compounds if the food is charred excessively.

Understanding and mastering dry heat cooking methods can significantly elevate your culinary repertoire. Baking offers a world of possibilities for both sweet and savory dishes, allowing for creative expression in the kitchen. Roasting brings out the best in meats and vegetables, enhancing their natural flavors and creating satisfying textures. Grilling, with its unique ability to infuse food with smoky flavors and produce enticing grill marks, is perfect for quick, flavorful meals. By learning to harness the power of dry heat, you can create delicious, healthy, and visually appealing dishes that will delight your senses and impress your guests.

Moist Heat Cooking Methods: Boiling, Steaming, Poaching

Moist heat cooking methods use water, steam, or broth to transfer heat to food, resulting in tender, flavorful dishes. These techniques are particularly well-suited for delicate foods and those that benefit from gentle cooking. The three primary moist heat methods are boiling, steaming, and poaching, each offering distinct advantages and applications in the kitchen.

Boiling

Boiling involves cooking food in water or broth that has been heated to its boiling point, typically 212°F (100°C) at sea level. This method is commonly used for cooking pasta, rice, vegetables, and legumes. Boiling is a straightforward and quick cooking technique, ideal for foods that need to be cooked thoroughly and evenly. The intense heat of boiling water rapidly cooks food, making it a time-efficient method. For vegetables, boiling can help retain their vibrant colors and preserve nutrients if done correctly and for the right amount of time. However, prolonged boiling can lead to nutrient loss, particularly of water-soluble vitamins like vitamin C and B vitamins. To minimize this, it is best to use the least amount of water needed and to save the cooking water for soups or sauces to recapture lost nutrients.

Steaming

Steaming involves cooking food by surrounding it with steam, which transfers heat to the food more gently than boiling. This method is excellent for vegetables, fish, and delicate items like dumplings and custards. Steaming helps retain the food's natural flavors, textures, and nutrients because the food never comes into direct contact with water. To steam effectively, place the food in a steamer basket or on a rack above boiling water, cover it with a lid to trap the steam, and cook until tender. The gentle heat of steam prevents overcooking and preserves the food's vibrant colors and nutritional content. Steaming is especially beneficial for vegetables, as it helps maintain their crisp-tender texture and bright colors, making it a healthy and visually appealing cooking method.

Poaching

Poaching is a method of cooking food gently in a liquid kept at a temperature just below boiling, usually between 160°F (71°C) and 180°F (82°C). The liquid can be water, broth, or a flavorful mixture of liquids and seasonings. Poaching is ideal for delicate foods that might fall apart or dry out under harsher cooking conditions, such as eggs, fish, and poultry. To poach, bring the liquid to the desired temperature, add the food, and cook it gently until done. The low temperature ensures that the food cooks slowly and evenly, resulting in a moist, tender texture. Poached dishes often have a subtle, delicate flavor, allowing the natural taste of the food to shine. For example, poached salmon retains its moisture and delicate flavor, while poached eggs have a tender white and runny yolk, perfect for dishes like Eggs Benedict.

Benefits and Considerations

Moist heat cooking methods offer several advantages. They are excellent for tenderizing tough cuts of meat, preserving the natural flavors and nutrients of food, and providing a moist, delicate texture. These methods are also versatile and can be adapted to a wide range of ingredients and dishes. However, it is essential to monitor the cooking process carefully to avoid overcooking, which can result in mushy textures and diminished flavors. Additionally, the temperature and cooking time must be adjusted based on the type and size of the food being cooked to achieve the best results.

Mastering moist heat cooking methods can greatly expand your culinary repertoire and improve the quality of your dishes. Boiling provides a quick and efficient way to cook a variety of foods, while steaming preserves nutrients and enhances the natural flavors and textures of ingredients. Poaching offers a gentle cooking option that is perfect for delicate foods, creating moist, tender dishes with subtle, nuanced flavors. By understanding and utilizing these moist heat techniques, you can create healthy, delicious meals that highlight the natural qualities of your ingredients. Whether you're preparing a simple vegetable side dish, a delicate poached fish, or a hearty bowl of pasta, these methods will help you achieve consistently excellent results in the kitchen.

Combination Cooking Methods: Braising, Stewing

Combination cooking methods, such as braising and stewing, combine dry and moist heat techniques to tenderize tough cuts of meat and create rich, flavorful dishes. These methods are well-suited for tougher cuts of meat that require long, slow cooking to break down connective tissues and develop deep flavors. Here, we explore the principles and techniques behind braising and stewing, highlighting their distinct characteristics and culinary applications.

Braising

Braising involves searing meat or vegetables in fat at high temperatures and then finishing them in a covered pot with a small amount of liquid. This method is typically used for larger cuts of meat like pot roast, short ribs, or brisket. The initial searing caramelizes the surface of the meat, known as the Maillard reaction, creating complex flavors and a rich brown crust. After searing, the meat is placed in a heavy-bottomed pot or Dutch oven with aromatic vegetables, herbs, and a small amount of liquid, such as broth. The pot is covered tightly, and the meat is cooked slowly at low temperatures in the oven or on the stovetop. The gentle heat and steam inside the pot break down tough connective tissues over time, transforming the meat into tender, succulent perfection. Braising not only tenderizes tougher cuts but also infuses them with the flavors of the cooking liquid and aromatics, creating a hearty, satisfying dish.

Stewing

Stewing is similar to braising but involves cutting food into smaller pieces and completely submerging them in liquid during cooking. This method is commonly used for making soups, stews, and casseroles using ingredients like meat, poultry, fish, vegetables, and legumes. Stewing allows flavors to meld together as the ingredients cook slowly in their own juices or a flavorful broth. The prolonged cooking time at low temperatures allows tough meats to become tender and vegetables to soften, while also allowing the flavors to develop and intensify. Stews and soups often benefit from extended cooking times, as they allow the ingredients to absorb the flavors of herbs, spices, and seasonings added to the pot. The resulting dishes are hearty, comforting, and deeply flavorful, making them ideal for cold weather or when feeding a crowd.

Benefits and Considerations

Combination cooking methods offer several benefits beyond tenderizing tough cuts of meat. They allow for the development of complex flavors and textures, making them ideal for creating comforting, satisfying dishes. These methods also make efficient use of less expensive cuts of meat, transforming them into delicious meals that rival more expensive cuts in flavor and tenderness. However, combination cooking methods require time and patience, as the slow cooking process is essential for achieving the desired results. It is important to monitor the cooking liquid to ensure it does not evaporate too quickly, which can lead to dry, tough meat or burnt flavors.

Braising and stewing are versatile and rewarding cooking methods that allow home cooks to create flavorful, tender dishes with relatively inexpensive ingredients. Whether you're simmering a pot of beef stew on the stove or braising a pot roast in the oven, these techniques transform tough cuts of meat and hearty vegetables into meals that are both delicious and comforting. By mastering the principles of combination cooking methods, you can expand your culinary repertoire and delight friends and family with savory, satisfying dishes year-round.

Salt, Herbs, And Spices

Salt, herbs, and spices are essential elements in cooking that elevate flavors, enhance aromas, and add complexity to dishes. Each plays a distinct role in seasoning food, balancing flavors, and creating memorable culinary experiences. Understanding how to effectively use salt, herbs, and spices can greatly enhance your cooking skills and the overall enjoyment of your meals.

Salt

Salt is perhaps the most fundamental seasoning in cooking, enhancing the natural flavors of ingredients and balancing sweetness and acidity. It not only adds a savory taste but also affects the texture and structure of food. When used in moderation, salt can amplify flavors without overpowering them. Different types of salt, such as kosher salt, sea salt, and table salt, have varying textures and flavors, influencing how they interact with food. Kosher salt, with its larger grains, is ideal for seasoning meats before cooking, while sea salt adds a subtle briny flavor and enhances the natural sweetness of vegetables. Table salt, with its fine texture, dissolves easily and is commonly used in baking and general cooking.

Herbs

Herbs are aromatic plants with leaves, stems, or flowers that are used fresh or dried to add flavor and aroma to dishes. Popular culinary herbs include basil, thyme, rosemary, parsley, cilantro, and mint, each offering unique flavors and complementing different types of cuisine. Fresh herbs are vibrant and add brightness to dishes, while dried herbs have a more concentrated flavor and are ideal for longer cooking times. Herbs can be used as a garnish, infused into oils and vinegars, or blended into sauces and marinades to enhance the overall flavor profile of a dish. Understanding the potency of herbs is essential; a little goes a long way, and their flavors can intensify during cooking, so it's best to add them gradually and taste as you go.

Spices

Spices are aromatic substances derived from seeds, roots, bark, or other parts of plants, often dried and ground into powder or used whole. They impart robust flavors, warmth, and complexity to dishes, making them essential in global cuisines. Common spices include cinnamon, cumin, paprika, ginger, turmeric, and chili powder, each bringing its distinctive character to dishes. Spices can be used to create depth in savory dishes, add warmth to desserts, or provide a kick of heat to spicy cuisines. Whole spices, when toasted and ground fresh, release their oils and intensify their flavors, enhancing the overall complexity of a dish.

Using Salt, Herbs, and Spices Together

Combining salt, herbs, and spices harmoniously can transform ordinary dishes into extraordinary culinary creations. The key to successful seasoning lies in balancing these elements to create a symphony of flavors. Start by seasoning with salt to enhance the natural flavors of ingredients. Then, layer in herbs and spices to add complexity and depth. For example, a simple roasted chicken can be seasoned with salt, fresh rosemary, and garlic powder before roasting to infuse it with savory flavors and aromas. Likewise, a vegetable stir-fry can be elevated with a combination of soy sauce for saltiness, fresh ginger for brightness, and red pepper flakes for heat.

Benefits and Considerations

Understanding how to use salt, herbs, and spices effectively allows you to tailor dishes to your taste preferences and create well-balanced meals. Experimenting with different combinations and proportions can enhance your culinary skills and expand your repertoire of flavors. However, it's essential to use these seasonings judiciously, as too much salt can overpower flavors, and excessive use of herbs and spices can overwhelm the palate. Start with small amounts, taste as you go, and adjust seasoning accordingly to achieve a harmonious balance of flavors.

Salt, herbs, and spices are indispensable tools in the kitchen, offering endless possibilities for enhancing flavors and creating memorable meals. By mastering the art of seasoning with salt, harnessing the freshness of herbs, and embracing the complexity of spices, you can elevate your cooking to new heights. Whether you're preparing a simple salad, a comforting stew, or an elaborate multi-course meal, these elements will serve as your guide to crafting delicious, well-balanced dishes that delight the senses and satisfy the soul.

Creating Flavor Profiles

Creating flavor profiles is an artful process in culinary exploration, where the combination of various tastes, textures, and aromas harmoniously balances and enhances the overall dining experience. Understanding how different ingredients interact and complement each other is key to crafting well-rounded dishes that appeal to the palate. Here's a detailed look at the principles and techniques involved in creating flavor profiles:

Understanding Flavor Components

Flavor in food is typically categorized into several components:

1. Basic Tastes: The basic tastes include sweet, salty, sour, bitter, and umami. Each taste adds a distinct dimension to dishes and can be adjusted to achieve balance.

2. Aromatics: Aromatics refer to the fragrant compounds in foods that contribute to their smell and taste. Common aromatics include herbs (like basil, thyme, and mint), spices (such as cinnamon, cumin, and ginger), and vegetables like onions, garlic, and peppers.

3. Textures: Texture plays a significant role in flavor perception. Crispy, crunchy, creamy, and chewy textures can influence how flavors are perceived and enjoyed.

4. Mouthfeel: Mouthfeel refers to the physical sensations experienced in the mouth, such as creaminess, viscosity, and astringency. It affects how flavors are perceived and enjoyed.

Building Blocks of Flavor

To create a balanced flavor profile, chefs often use the following building blocks:

1. Base Flavors: Start with a foundation of flavors that form the core of the dish. This could be the natural sweetness of vegetables, the umami richness of meat or mushrooms, or the creamy texture of dairy.

2. Contrast: Introduce contrasting flavors to add complexity and interest. For example, pair sweet with salty or sour with spicy to create a dynamic flavor experience.

3. Layering: Layer flavors by adding ingredients at different stages of cooking or preparation. This allows flavors to meld together while maintaining their distinct characteristics.

4. Harmonization: Aim for harmony among flavors by balancing sweet, salty, sour, bitter, and umami tastes. Adjust seasoning and ingredients to achieve a pleasing balance.

Techniques for Creating Flavor Profiles

1. Sauteing and Searing: Browning meats and vegetables enhances their natural flavors through the Maillard reaction, creating depth and complexity.

2. Deglazing: Adding liquid (such as broth, or vinegar) to a pan after sauteing helps to release flavorful browned bits and creates a rich sauce.

3. Reduction: Simmering liquids like stocks or sauces intensifies flavors by concentrating their natural essences.

4. Marinating: Allowing proteins or vegetables to soak in a seasoned liquid (like oil, vinegar, or yogurt) before cooking infuses them with flavor.

5. Seasoning: Using salt, herbs, and spices judiciously throughout cooking enhances and balances flavors.

Examples of Flavor Profiles

1. Mediterranean: Olive oil, garlic, tomatoes, basil, oregano, and lemon create fresh, herbaceous flavors with a hint of tanginess.

2. Asian: Soy sauce, ginger, garlic, sesame oil, and chili peppers combine savory, sweet, and spicy elements for a bold, umami-rich profile.

3. Mexican: Cumin, chili powder, cilantro, lime, and jalapenos blend earthy, spicy, and citrusy flavors with a touch of heat.

Benefits and Considerations

Creating well-crafted flavor profiles allows chefs to showcase ingredients' natural qualities and create dishes that are balanced, nuanced, and memorable. However, it requires experimentation, creativity, and an understanding of ingredient interactions. Balancing flavors ensures that no single taste dominates, creating a harmonious and enjoyable eating experience.

Mastering the art of creating flavor profiles is fundamental to elevating your culinary skills and delighting diners with delicious, well-balanced dishes. By understanding the components of flavor, experimenting with building blocks, and employing various cooking techniques, you can develop your unique culinary style and create dishes that captivate the senses and leave a lasting impression. Whether you're preparing a simple meal or a gourmet feast, crafting thoughtful flavor profiles will transform your cooking into a creative and rewarding culinary journey.

Marinades, Rubs, and Brines

Marinades, rubs, and brines are versatile techniques used to enhance flavors, tenderize meats, and infuse ingredients with seasonings before cooking. Each method offers distinct benefits and can be tailored to suit different types of food, cooking styles, and flavor preferences. Here's an exploration of marinades, rubs, and brines, along with their applications and advantages in culinary practices:

Marinades

Marinades are flavorful liquids in which food is soaked before cooking, typically for several hours or overnight. They serve multiple purposes, including adding flavor, tenderizing tougher cuts of meat, and sometimes preserving ingredients. Marinades typically contain an acidic component like vinegar, citrus juice, or yogurt, which helps break down proteins and connective tissues, resulting in more tender and flavorful dishes. Oil is often included to help distribute flavors and prevent food from sticking during cooking.

Marinades can be simple, comprising basic ingredients like olive oil, vinegar, garlic, herbs, and spices, or more complex with additional components such as soy sauce, honey. The choice of ingredients depends on the desired flavor profile and the type of dish being prepared. For example, a citrus-based marinade with lime juice, garlic, and cilantro is ideal for chicken or fish, imparting a zesty, fresh taste.

Rubs

Rubs consist of dry seasonings, such as herbs, spices, salt, and sugar that are applied directly to the surface of food before cooking. Unlike marinades, rubs create a flavorful crust on the exterior of meats or vegetables, enhancing both taste and texture. Rubs are particularly well-suited for grilling, roasting, or smoking, as they create a caramelized, crispy exterior while sealing in juices and flavors.

To apply a rub, simply coat the food evenly with the dry mixture, pressing it into the surface to ensure adherence. Allow the rubbed food to rest for some time before cooking to allow the flavors to penetrate. Common ingredients in rubs include paprika, cumin, garlic powder, brown sugar, and black pepper, each contributing to a robust, aromatic profile.

Brines

Brining involves soaking food in a saltwater solution, known as a brine, before cooking. The primary purpose of brining is to enhance moisture retention and flavor absorption, particularly for lean meats like poultry and lamb that tend to dry out during cooking. Brines also help to tenderize proteins by altering their structure and breaking down muscle fibers, resulting in juicier, more flavorful dishes.

A basic brine consists of water, salt, and often sugar or other sweeteners, along with aromatics such as herbs, garlic, and spices. The salt concentration is crucial, as it affects how much water the food absorbs. Brining times vary based on the size and type of food, ranging from a few hours for chicken breasts to several days for large cuts of meat or whole turkeys. After brining, rinse the food thoroughly to remove excess salt and pat it dry before cooking.

Benefits and Considerations

Each of these techniques offers distinct benefits in enhancing flavor and texture:

- **Marinades** infuse food with complex flavors and help tenderize tougher cuts.

- **Rubs** create flavorful crusts and enhance the texture of grilled or roasted foods.

- **Brines** improve moisture retention and tenderness, particularly in lean meats.

However, it's essential to consider factors such as marinating times, ingredient proportions, and cooking methods to achieve optimal results. Over-marinating can lead to mushy textures or overly intense flavors, while under-marinating may not sufficiently enhance taste or tenderize meat.

Marinades, rubs, and brines are valuable techniques in culinary arts, offering creative ways to enhance flavors, tenderize meats, and elevate dishes. By experimenting with different ingredients, proportions, and application methods, chefs and home cooks alike can personalize their cooking and create dishes that are flavorful, juicy, and memorable. Whether preparing a simple weeknight meal or hosting a special gathering, mastering these techniques can transform ordinary ingredients into extraordinary culinary creations that delight the senses and satisfy the palate.

PART 2: BREAKFAST AND BRUNCH

Start your day right with enticing breakfast and brunch recipes that cater to every palate. From fluffy omelets and classic pancakes to homemade bread and nutritious smoothies, this section offers delicious morning inspirations that promise to make your breakfasts the highlight of your day.

1) Perfect Scrambled Eggs

Ingredients:

- 4 large eggs
- Salt and freshly ground black pepper, to taste
- 2 tablespoons whole milk or heavy cream (optional)
- 1 tablespoon unsalted butter
- Chopped fresh chives or parsley, for garnish (optional)

Instructions:

1. **Preparation:** Crack the eggs into a mixing bowl. Season with salt and pepper to taste. If using, add the milk or cream to the eggs and whisk everything together until well combined and slightly frothy.

2. **Heat the Pan:** Place a non-stick skillet or frying pan over medium-low heat. Add the butter and allow it to melt completely, swirling the pan to coat the bottom evenly.

3. **Cooking the Eggs:** Once the butter is melted and slightly bubbling, pour the egg mixture into the skillet. Let it sit undisturbed for about 10-15 seconds until the edges begin to set.

4. **Stirring:** Using a spatula or wooden spoon, gently stir the eggs from the edges towards the center of the pan. Allow the uncooked eggs to flow into the empty spaces. Continue to stir and fold the eggs gently, scraping the bottom and sides of the pan, until the eggs form soft, creamy curds. This should take about 2-3 minutes.

5. **Adjusting Heat:** If the eggs are cooking too quickly, reduce the heat to low to ensure they cook gently and evenly. The eggs should be creamy with no runny liquid remaining.

6. **Finishing:** Remove the pan from the heat just before the eggs are fully cooked, as they will continue to cook from residual heat. The texture should be soft and slightly glossy.

7. **Serving:** Transfer the scrambled eggs to a warm plate immediately. Garnish with chopped fresh chives or parsley if desired. Serve hot with toast, crispy bacon, or smoked salmon.

Tips for Perfect Scrambled Eggs:

- Use fresh, high-quality eggs for the best flavor and texture.

- Avoid overcooking the eggs; they should be soft and creamy, not dry or rubbery.

- Experiment with additions like cheese, herbs, or sautéed vegetables to customize your scrambled eggs.

Enjoy these perfect scrambled eggs for a delicious breakfast or brunch, served with your favorite sides for a satisfying start to the day!

2) Fluffy Omelet

Creating a fluffy omelet requires careful technique and attention to detail to achieve a light, airy texture with a creamy interior. Here's a step-by-step recipe to make a perfect fluffy omelet:

Ingredients:

- 3 large eggs
- Salt and freshly ground black pepper, to taste
- 1 tablespoon unsalted butter
- Fillings of your choice (e.g., cheese, ham, vegetables, herbs)

Instructions:

1. **Prepare Fillings:** If using fillings like cheese, ham, or vegetables, prepare them ahead of time by chopping or grating as needed.

2. **Whisk Eggs:** Crack the eggs into a bowl. Season with salt and pepper to taste. Whisk vigorously with a fork or whisk until the yolks and whites are fully combined and slightly frothy.

3. **Heat the Pan:** Place a non-stick skillet or frying pan over medium-low heat. Add the butter and allow it to melt completely, swirling the pan to coat the bottom evenly.

4. **Cooking the Omelet:**

    - Once the butter is melted and slightly bubbling, pour the whisked eggs into the skillet.

    - Let the eggs sit undisturbed for about 10-15 seconds until the edges begin to set.

5. **Folding the Omelet:** Using a spatula, gently push the edges of the omelet towards the center, tilting the pan to let any uncooked eggs flow to the edges. Continue this process around the entire omelet until it is mostly set but still slightly runny on top.

6. **Adding Fillings:** Sprinkle your chosen fillings evenly over one half of the omelet. This can include grated cheese, diced ham, sautéed vegetables, or fresh herbs.

7. **Finishing the Omelet:**

- Carefully fold the empty half of the omelet over the fillings using the spatula.
- Press gently with the spatula to seal the omelet and shape it into a half-moon.

8. **Final Cooking:** Cook the omelet for another 1-2 minutes, allowing the fillings to heat through and the eggs to finish cooking. The omelet should be fluffy and slightly puffed.

9. **Serve:** Slide the fluffy omelet onto a warm plate. Garnish with fresh herbs or a sprinkle of cheese if desired. Serve immediately while hot.

Tips for a Perfect Fluffy Omelet:

- Use a non-stick skillet or frying pan to prevent the omelet from sticking and ensure easy flipping.
- Cook the omelet over medium-low heat to avoid overcooking and maintain a fluffy texture.
- Experiment with different fillings to create variations in flavor and texture.

Mastering the art of making a fluffy omelet takes practice, but with these steps and tips, you'll be able to create a delicious and satisfying breakfast or brunch dish that's sure to impress!

3) Classic Pancakes and Waffles

Pancakes and waffles are beloved breakfast staples enjoyed for their fluffy texture and versatility in pairing with various toppings. Here's how to make classic pancakes and waffles from scratch, ensuring delicious results every time:

Classic Pancakes

Ingredients:

- 1 cup all-purpose flour
- 2 tablespoons granulated sugar
- 1 teaspoon baking powder
- 1/2 teaspoon baking soda
- 1/4 teaspoon salt
- 3/4 cup buttermilk (or 3/4 cup milk mixed with 1 tablespoon lemon juice or vinegar)
- 1/4 cup milk
- 1 large egg
- 2 tablespoons unsalted butter, melted
- 1 teaspoon vanilla extract (optional)
- Butter or oil for cooking

Instructions:

1. **Preparation:** In a mixing bowl, whisk together the flour, sugar, baking powder, baking soda, and salt until well combined.

2. **Mixing Batter:** In another bowl, whisk together the buttermilk, milk, egg, melted butter, and vanilla extract (if using) until smooth.

3. **Combine Ingredients:** Pour the wet ingredients into the dry ingredients and stir gently until just combined. Be careful not to overmix; a few lumps are okay. Let the batter rest for about 5-10 minutes to allow the baking powder and baking soda to activate.

4. **Cooking Pancakes:** Heat a non-stick skillet or griddle over medium heat. Add a small amount of butter or oil and swirl to coat the surface. Pour about 1/4 cup of batter onto the skillet for each pancake, spacing them apart.

5. **Cooking Process:** Cook until bubbles form on the surface of the pancakes and the edges look set, about 2-3 minutes. Flip the pancakes and cook for an additional 1-2 minutes until golden brown and cooked through.

6. **Serve:** Transfer the pancakes to a plate and keep warm. Repeat with the remaining batter, adding more butter or oil to the skillet as needed. Serve the pancakes warm with butter, maple syrup, fresh fruits, or other toppings of your choice.

Classic Waffles

Ingredients:

- 1 3/4 cups all-purpose flour
- 2 tablespoons granulated sugar
- 1 tablespoon baking powder
- 1/2 teaspoon salt
- 2 large eggs
- 1 3/4 cups milk
- 1/2 cup unsalted butter, melted
- 1 teaspoon vanilla extract (optional)
- Butter or oil for greasing waffle iron

Instructions:

1. **Preparation:** Preheat your waffle iron according to manufacturer's instructions.
2. **Mixing Batter:** In a mixing bowl, whisk together the flour, sugar, baking powder, and salt until well combined.
3. **Combine Ingredients:** In another bowl, whisk together the eggs, milk, melted butter, and vanilla extract (if using) until smooth.

4. **Mix Batter:** Pour the wet ingredients into the dry ingredients and stir gently until just combined. Be careful not to overmix; a few lumps are okay.

5. **Cooking Waffles:** Lightly grease the waffle iron with butter or oil. Pour enough batter onto the preheated waffle iron to cover the grids. Close the lid and cook according to the manufacturer's instructions until golden brown and crispy.

6. **Serve:** Carefully remove the waffle from the iron and serve immediately, or keep warm in a low oven until ready to serve. Serve the waffles with butter, maple syrup, fresh berries, whipped cream, or other toppings of your choice.

Tips for Perfect Pancakes and Waffles:

- For lighter pancakes and waffles, avoid overmixing the batter. Stir until just combined to prevent dense textures.

- Adjust the thickness of the batter by adding more milk for thinner pancakes or waffles, or more flour for thicker ones.

- Keep the pancakes and waffles warm by placing them in a single layer on a baking sheet in a low oven (around 200°F / 95°C) while finishing the rest.

Enjoy these classic pancakes and waffles for a delightful breakfast or brunch, perfect for any occasion!

4) Homemade Bread and Rolls

Homemade bread and rolls are a rewarding culinary endeavor, offering the satisfaction of freshly baked goods with delightful aromas filling the kitchen. Here's a step-by-step guide to making delicious homemade bread and rolls:

Homemade Bread

Ingredients:

- 3 1/2 cups all-purpose flour
- 1 packet (2 1/4 teaspoons) active dry yeast
- 1 cup warm water (about 110°F or 45°C)
- 2 tablespoons granulated sugar
- 1 teaspoon salt
- 2 tablespoons unsalted butter, melted
- Additional flour for dusting

Instructions:

1. **Activate Yeast:** In a small bowl, combine the warm water, sugar, and yeast. Stir gently and let it sit for about 5-10 minutes until the mixture

becomes frothy and bubbly, indicating that the yeast is active.

2. **Mix Dough:** In a large mixing bowl, combine the flour and salt. Make a well in the center and pour in the activated yeast mixture and melted butter.

3. **Knead Dough:** Stir the ingredients together until a dough begins to form. Transfer the dough onto a lightly floured surface and knead for about 8-10 minutes until the dough is smooth, elastic, and no longer sticky. Add more flour as needed to prevent sticking.

4. **First Rise:** Place the dough in a lightly greased bowl, cover with a clean kitchen towel or plastic wrap, and let it rise in a warm, draft-free place for about 1-1.5 hours or until doubled in size.

5. **Shape and Second Rise:** Punch down the risen dough to release air bubbles. Divide the dough into equal portions for loaves or rolls. Shape each portion into desired shapes (loaves, round rolls, braids, etc.) and place them on a parchment-lined baking sheet. Cover again and let them rise for another 30-45 minutes until puffed up.

6. **Preheat Oven:** Preheat the oven to 375°F (190°C). Optionally, you can brush the risen loaves or rolls with melted butter for a shiny finish.

7. **Bake:** Bake the bread or rolls in the preheated oven for 20-25 minutes (for rolls) or 30-35 minutes (for loaves), or until they are golden brown on top and sound hollow when tapped on the bottom.

8. **Cool and Serve:** Remove the baked bread or rolls from the oven and let them cool on a wire rack before slicing or serving. Enjoy warm with butter or your favorite toppings.

Tips for Homemade Bread:

- Ensure the water used to activate the yeast is warm but not too hot (around 110°F / 45°C). Hot water can kill the yeast, while cold water won't activate it properly.

- Kneading the dough develops gluten, which gives bread its structure and elasticity. Knead until the dough is smooth and elastic.

- Let the dough rise in a warm, draft-free place for the best results. The first rise allows the yeast to ferment and create carbon dioxide, which gives the bread its airy texture.

Homemade Rolls

Ingredients:

- Same ingredients as for homemade bread

- Additional melted butter for brushing (optional)

Instructions:

- Follow the same steps as for homemade bread, but after shaping the dough into rolls, place them closer together on a baking sheet for a softer side.

Enjoy the process of baking homemade bread and rolls, filling your home with the aroma of freshly baked goods and savoring the delicious results with family and friends.

5) Savory and Sweet Pastries

Pastries come in a delightful variety of flavors and textures, ranging from savory to sweet, and they make for perfect treats any time of day. Here's how to prepare both savory and sweet pastries to satisfy different cravings:

Savory Pastries: Spinach and Feta Puffs

Ingredients:

- 1 package (17.3 ounces) puff pastry sheets, thawed
- 1 cup frozen chopped spinach, thawed and squeezed dry
- 1 cup crumbled feta cheese

- 1/4 cup grated Parmesan cheese
- 1/4 teaspoon garlic powder
- Salt and pepper, to taste
- 1 egg, beaten (for egg wash)

Instructions:

1. **Preheat Oven:** Preheat your oven to 400°F (200°C). Line a baking sheet with parchment paper.

2. **Prepare Filling:** In a mixing bowl, combine the chopped spinach, feta cheese, Parmesan cheese, garlic powder, salt, and pepper. Mix well until evenly combined.

3. **Roll out Pastry:** On a lightly floured surface, unfold one sheet of puff pastry. Roll it out slightly to smooth any creases and make it slightly thinner.

4. **Cut Pastry:** Cut the puff pastry sheet into squares or rectangles, depending on the size of pastries desired.

5. **Fill Pastries:** Place a spoonful of the spinach and feta mixture in the center of each pastry square. Fold the corners of each square toward the center, overlapping slightly to seal the filling

inside. Press the edges with a fork to seal them further.

6. **Egg Wash:** Place the pastries on the prepared baking sheet. Brush the tops of the pastries with beaten egg for a golden finish.

7. **Bake:** Bake in the preheated oven for 15-18 minutes, or until the pastries are puffed and golden brown.

8. **Serve:** Remove from the oven and let cool slightly on a wire rack before serving. Enjoy warm as a delicious appetizer or snack.

Sweet Pastries: Apple Turnovers

Ingredients:

- 1 package (17.3 ounces) puff pastry sheets, thawed
- 2 large apples, peeled, cored, and diced
- 2 tablespoons unsalted butter
- 1/4 cup granulated sugar
- 1/2 teaspoon ground cinnamon
- 1/4 teaspoon ground nutmeg
- 1 tablespoon all-purpose flour

- 1 egg, beaten (for egg wash)
- Powdered sugar, for dusting (optional)

Instructions:

1. **Preheat Oven:** Preheat your oven to 400°F (200°C). Line a baking sheet with parchment paper.

2. **Prepare Filling:** In a skillet, melt the butter over medium heat. Add the diced apples, granulated sugar, cinnamon, and nutmeg. Cook, stirring occasionally, until the apples are tender and caramelized, about 5-7 minutes. Stir in the flour and cook for another minute until thickened. Remove from heat and let cool slightly.

3. **Roll out Pastry:** On a lightly floured surface, unfold one sheet of puff pastry. Roll it out slightly to smooth any creases and make it slightly thinner.

4. **Cut Pastry:** Cut the puff pastry sheet into squares or rectangles, depending on the size of turnovers desired.

5. **Fill and Fold:** Place a spoonful of the apple filling in the center of each pastry square. Fold the pastry over the filling to form a triangle. Press the edges with a fork to seal them. Repeat with the remaining pastry and filling.

6. **Egg Wash:** Place the turnovers on the prepared baking sheet. Brush the tops of the turnovers with beaten egg for a shiny finish.

7. **Bake:** Bake in the preheated oven for 15-18 minutes, or until the turnovers are puffed and golden brown.

8. **Serve:** Remove from the oven and let cool slightly on a wire rack. Dust with powdered sugar before serving, if desired. Enjoy warm as a delightful dessert or sweet treat.

Tips for Savory and Sweet Pastries:

- Use high-quality puff pastry for the best results. Thaw it according to package instructions before use.

- Customize the fillings to your taste preferences. For savory pastries, try different combinations of cheeses, vegetables, or meats. For sweet pastries, experiment with different fruits and spices.

- Serve pastries warm for the best flavor and texture, whether as appetizers, snacks, or desserts. They can also be reheated briefly in the oven to restore crispness.

Enjoy making these savory and sweet pastries to impress your family and guests, whether for brunch, parties, or everyday indulgence!

6) Fresh Juices and Smoothies

Fresh juices and smoothies are refreshing beverages packed with nutrients, ideal for a quick breakfast, a post-workout boost, or a healthy snack. Here's how to create delicious and nutritious fresh juices and smoothies at home:

Fresh Juices: Orange Carrot Ginger Juice

Ingredients:

- 4 large carrots, washed and peeled
- 3 large oranges, peeled
- 1-inch piece of fresh ginger, peeled
- Optional: honey or agave syrup, to taste
- Ice cubes (optional)

Instructions:

1. **Prepare Ingredients:** Cut the carrots and oranges into smaller pieces that will fit into your juicer chute. Cut the ginger into smaller chunks.

2. **Juicing Process:** Feed the carrots, oranges, and ginger through a juicer according to the manufacturer's instructions. Ensure that the juicer extracts all the juice from the ingredients.

3. **Optional Sweetener:** Taste the juice and add honey or agave syrup if desired, depending on your sweetness preference. Stir well to combine.

4. **Serve:** Pour the freshly made juice into glasses over ice cubes if desired. Serve immediately to enjoy the fresh flavor and nutrients.

Smoothies: Berry Banana Spinach Smoothie

Ingredients:

- 1 cup fresh spinach leaves, washed
- 1 ripe banana, peeled and sliced
- 1/2 cup mixed berries (such as strawberries, blueberries, raspberries)
- 1/2 cup plain yogurt or Greek yogurt
- 1/2 cup milk (dairy or plant-based)
- Optional: honey or maple syrup, to taste
- Ice cubes (optional)

Instructions:

1. **Blend Ingredients:** In a blender, combine the spinach leaves, banana slices, mixed berries, yogurt, and milk.

2. **Blend until Smooth:** Blend on high speed until smooth and creamy. Add more milk if needed to reach your desired consistency.

3. **Optional Sweetener:** Taste the smoothie and add honey or maple syrup if desired for added sweetness. Blend again briefly to incorporate.

4. **Serve:** Pour the smoothie into glasses. Add ice cubes if you prefer a colder drink. Serve immediately for the best flavor and texture.

Tips for Fresh Juices and Smoothies:

- Use fresh, ripe fruits and vegetables for the best flavor and nutrient content.

- Customize your juices and smoothies by adding ingredients like spinach, kale, celery, or herbs for additional nutritional benefits.

- Experiment with different flavor combinations and ratios of ingredients to suit your taste preferences.

- Clean your juicer or blender promptly after use to maintain its performance and prolong its lifespan.

Enjoy the vibrant flavors and health benefits of these fresh juices and smoothies as part of your balanced diet and wellness routine!

7) Coffee and Tea Variations

Coffee and tea are versatile beverages enjoyed worldwide for their diverse flavors, aromas, and cultural significance. Here's a look at various coffee and tea variations, each offering unique characteristics and methods of preparation:

Coffee Variations

1. Espresso: Espresso is a concentrated coffee brewed by forcing a small amount of nearly boiling water through finely-ground coffee beans. It has a rich flavor and a layer of crema on top, often served in small shots.

2. Cappuccino: Cappuccino consists of equal parts espresso, steamed milk, and milk foam. It has a balanced flavor with a creamy texture and is often topped with a sprinkle of cocoa powder or cinnamon.

3. Latte: Latte is made with espresso and steamed milk, usually in a 1:3 ratio (one part espresso to three parts milk). It has a smooth, creamy texture and can be flavored with syrups like vanilla or caramel.

4. Americano: Americano is made by diluting a shot of espresso with hot water, giving it a similar strength to drip coffee but with a different flavor profile. It has a lighter body and is often enjoyed black or with a splash of milk.

5. Macchiato: Macchiato translates to "stained" or "spotted" in Italian. It's an espresso "stained" with a small amount of steamed milk or milk foam, providing a strong coffee flavor with a touch of creaminess.

Tea Variations

1. Green Tea: Green tea is made from unoxidized tea leaves, preserving its natural antioxidants and delicate flavor. It has a grassy, vegetal taste and is often enjoyed plain or with a slice of lemon.

2. Black Tea: Black tea undergoes full oxidation, resulting in a robust flavor with hints of malt or fruitiness, depending on the variety. It's commonly served with milk and sugar or enjoyed plain.

3. Herbal Tea: Herbal teas are caffeine-free infusions made from herbs, flowers, fruits, or spices. Popular varieties include chamomile, peppermint, and hibiscus, each offering unique health benefits and flavors.

4. Chai Tea: Chai tea is a spiced black tea beverage originating from India. It's brewed with black tea leaves, milk, sugar, and a blend of aromatic spices such as cardamom, cinnamon, ginger, cloves, and pepper.

5. Earl Grey Tea: Earl Grey tea is a flavored black tea infused with bergamot oil, giving it a distinctive citrusy aroma and flavor. It's often served plain or with a splash of milk.

Preparation Methods

- **Coffee:** Brewed using various methods like espresso machines, drip coffee makers, French press, or pour-over. Espresso-based drinks involve steaming milk and foam for added texture.

- **Tea:** Prepared by steeping tea leaves or bags in hot water for a specific time, typically 3-5 minutes for black tea and less for green or herbal teas. Some teas benefit from longer steeping times for stronger flavor.

Serving and Enjoyment

- **Coffee:** Enjoyed hot or cold, often accompanied by pastries or desserts. Specialty coffee shops offer a range of creative flavors and brewing methods.

- **Tea:** Served hot in ceramic or glass cups, often paired with scones, biscuits, or sandwiches. Iced tea variations are popular in warmer climates or as refreshing alternatives.

Whether you prefer the bold intensity of espresso or the soothing warmth of herbal tea, these beverages cater to diverse tastes and occasions, enriching culinary experiences around the world.

PART 3: APPETIZERS AND SNACKS

Elevate your hosting skills with an array of appetizers and snacks that are perfect for any occasion. From crispy vegetable samosas and flavorful meatballs to creamy hummus and zesty dips, these recipes are designed to impress and satisfy guests, whether for a casual gathering or a festive celebration.

8) Vegetable Samosas

Vegetable samosas are popular savory pastries originating from the Indian subcontinent, known for their crispy exterior and flavorful fillings. Here's how to make delicious vegetable samosas at home:

Ingredients:

For the Dough:

- 2 cups all-purpose flour
- 1/2 teaspoon salt
- 1/4 cup vegetable oil or melted ghee
- Water, as needed

For the Filling:

- 2 large potatoes, boiled, peeled, and diced
- 1 cup green peas, fresh or frozen
- 1 medium onion, finely chopped
- 1 green chili, finely chopped (optional)
- 1 teaspoon cumin seeds
- 1 teaspoon mustard seeds
- 1 teaspoon garam masala

- 1/2 teaspoon turmeric powder
- 1/2 teaspoon ground coriander
- 1/2 teaspoon ground cumin
- Salt, to taste
- Fresh cilantro leaves, chopped
- 2 tablespoons vegetable oil for cooking

For Frying:

- Vegetable oil, for deep frying

Instructions:

1. Prepare the Dough:

- In a large mixing bowl, combine the flour and salt. Add the vegetable oil or melted ghee and mix well until the mixture resembles breadcrumbs.
- Gradually add water, a little at a time, and knead into a smooth, firm dough. Cover the dough with a damp cloth and let it rest for 30 minutes.

2. Prepare the Filling:

- Heat 2 tablespoons of vegetable oil in a large skillet over medium heat. Add the cumin seeds and mustard seeds. When they start to splutter, add the chopped onion and green chili (if using). Sauté until the onion becomes translucent.

- Add the boiled and diced potatoes and green peas to the skillet. Stir in the garam masala, turmeric powder, ground coriander, ground cumin, and salt to taste. Mix well to combine all the spices with the vegetables. Cook for 5-7 minutes, stirring occasionally, until the peas are tender. Remove from heat and let the filling cool to room temperature. Stir in chopped fresh cilantro.

3. **Shape and Fill the Samosas:**

    - Divide the rested dough into equal-sized balls, about golf ball-sized portions. Roll each ball into a smooth ball and flatten it slightly with your palms.

    - Roll out each portion of dough into a circle of about 6-7 inches in diameter. Cut each circle in half to form two semi-circles.

    - Take one semi-circle of dough and fold it into a cone shape, sealing the edges with a little water. Hold the cone in your palm and fill it with 2-3 tablespoons of the cooled vegetable filling. Press the filling gently into the cone.

    - Seal the top of the cone by folding over the edges and pinching them together to form a triangular shape. Ensure the samosa is sealed tightly to prevent the filling from spilling out during frying. Repeat with the remaining dough and filling.

4. Fry the Samosas:

- Heat vegetable oil in a deep frying pan or kadhai over medium heat. Once the oil is hot (about 350°F / 180°C), carefully slide in a few samosas, ensuring not to overcrowd the pan.

- Fry the samosas for 6-8 minutes, turning occasionally, until they are golden brown and crispy. Use a slotted spoon to remove the fried samosas and place them on a plate lined with paper towels to drain excess oil.

5. Serve:

- Serve the vegetable samosas hot with mint chutney, tamarind chutney, or ketchup. Enjoy these crispy and flavorful snacks as an appetizer or part of a meal.

Tips for Making Vegetable Samosas:

- Ensure the dough is rolled out thin but not too thin to prevent the samosas from bursting during frying.

- Adjust the spiciness of the filling by adding more or fewer green chilies according to your preference.

- If preferred, you can bake the samosas in a preheated oven at 375°F (190°C) for 25-30 minutes, brushing them with oil or butter before baking.

Homemade vegetable samosas are a delicious treat, perfect for sharing with family and friends during gatherings or as a flavorful snack any time of day.

9) Meatballs

Meatballs are versatile, savory balls of ground meat mixed with seasonings and often served in various sauces or as appetizers. Here's how to make classic meatballs that are tender, flavorful, and perfect for any occasion:

Ingredients:

For the Meatballs:

- 1 pound ground beef (or a mix of beef and lamb)
- 1/2 cup breadcrumbs
- 1/4 cup grated Parmesan cheese
- 1/4 cup milk
- 1 egg
- 2 cloves garlic, minced

- 1 tablespoon fresh parsley, finely chopped (or 1 teaspoon dried parsley)
- 1 teaspoon salt
- 1/2 teaspoon black pepper
- 1/2 teaspoon dried oregano
- 1/4 teaspoon red pepper flakes (optional)
- 2 tablespoons olive oil, for cooking

For the Sauce (Optional):

- 2 cups marinara sauce or your favorite tomato sauce
- Fresh basil leaves, chopped (optional)

Instructions:

1. Prepare the Meatball Mixture:

- In a large mixing bowl, combine the breadcrumbs and milk. Let it sit for a few minutes until the breadcrumbs absorb the milk.
- Add the ground beef, grated Parmesan cheese, egg, minced garlic, chopped parsley, salt, black pepper, dried oregano, and red pepper flakes (if using) to the bowl with the breadcrumb mixture.

- Using your hands, gently mix all the ingredients together until well combined. Be careful not to overmix, as this can make the meatballs tough.

2. Shape the Meatballs:

- With clean hands, scoop about 1-2 tablespoons of the meat mixture and roll it between your palms to form a smooth ball. Repeat until all the mixture is used, placing the formed meatballs on a plate or baking sheet.

- You can adjust the size of the meatballs according to your preference, typically they are about 1 to 1.5 inches in diameter.

3. Cook the Meatballs:

- Heat olive oil in a large skillet over medium heat. Once the oil is hot, add the meatballs in a single layer, making sure not to overcrowd the skillet. You may need to cook them in batches.

- Cook the meatballs for about 4-5 minutes on each side, or until they are browned on all sides and cooked through. Use a spatula or tongs to gently turn them to avoid breaking.

4. Serve:

- If making sauce, add the marinara or tomato sauce to the skillet with the cooked meatballs. Gently stir to coat the meatballs in the sauce.

- Simmer the meatballs in the sauce for another 5-10 minutes, allowing them to absorb the flavors of the sauce. If desired, sprinkle chopped fresh basil over the meatballs before serving.

- Serve the meatballs hot as an appetizer, over pasta, with crusty bread, or as part of a meal. They also make delicious meatball subs or sliders.

Tips for Making Meatballs:

- **Mixing the Ingredients:** Mix the meatball mixture gently with your hands just until combined. Overmixing can lead to dense and tough meatballs.

- **Consistency:** If the mixture feels too wet and sticky, add a little more breadcrumbs. If it's too dry, add a splash more milk or a tablespoon of water.

- **Cooking:** Browning the meatballs before adding them to the sauce adds flavor and texture. Ensure they are cooked through by cutting one open to check or using a meat thermometer (internal temperature should reach 160°F / 71°C).

- **Sauce Options:** Experiment with different sauces like Swedish meatball sauce, barbecue sauce, or creamy mushroom sauce for variety.

Homemade meatballs are a comforting and versatile dish that can be customized with various seasonings and sauces to suit your taste preferences. Enjoy these tender and flavorful meatballs as a satisfying meal or appetizer!

10) *Dips and Spreads: Hummus and Baba Ganoush*

Dips and spreads are versatile additions to any meal or snack, offering rich flavors and textures that complement various dishes. Here's how to prepare classic Middle Eastern dips, hummus, and baba ganoush, each with its unique ingredients and method:

Hummus

Ingredients:

- 1 can (15 ounces) chickpeas, drained and rinsed
- 1/4 cup tahini (sesame paste)
- 1/4 cup fresh lemon juice (about 1 large lemon)
- 1-2 cloves garlic, minced
- 2-3 tablespoons extra virgin olive oil
- 1/2 teaspoon ground cumin
- Salt, to taste

- Water, as needed
- Paprika and olive oil, for garnish

Instructions:

1. **Prepare Chickpeas:** If using canned chickpeas, drain and rinse them thoroughly under cold water to remove excess salt and starch.

2. **Blend Ingredients:** In a food processor or blender, combine the chickpeas, tahini, lemon juice, minced garlic, cumin, and a pinch of salt. Pulse until the mixture becomes a coarse paste.

3. **Add Olive Oil and Water:** With the food processor running, gradually add the olive oil in a steady stream. If the hummus is too thick, add water, 1 tablespoon at a time, until you reach your desired consistency. Continue blending until smooth and creamy.

4. **Adjust Seasoning:** Taste the hummus and adjust the seasoning with more salt or lemon juice if needed. Blend again briefly to incorporate.

5. **Serve:** Transfer the hummus to a serving bowl. Drizzle with extra virgin olive oil and sprinkle with paprika for garnish. Serve with pita bread, vegetables, or as a spread in sandwiches.

Baba Ganoush

Ingredients:

- 2 large eggplants
- 1/4 cup tahini (sesame paste)
- 1/4 cup fresh lemon juice (about 1 large lemon)
- 2-3 cloves garlic, minced
- 2 tablespoons extra virgin olive oil
- Salt, to taste
- Fresh parsley, chopped, for garnish
- Optional: pomegranate seeds or sumac for garnish

Instructions:

1. **Roast the Eggplants:** Preheat the oven to 400°F (200°C). Prick the eggplants with a fork in several places and place them on a baking sheet. Roast in the oven for 45-60 minutes, turning occasionally, until the eggplants are very tender and collapsed. Remove from the oven and let cool.

2. **Prepare Eggplant Flesh:** Once cooled, peel off the skin of the eggplants and discard. Place the flesh in a colander to drain excess liquid for about 10 minutes.

3. **Blend Ingredients:** In a food processor or blender, combine the eggplant flesh, tahini, lemon juice, minced garlic, and olive oil. Pulse until smooth and creamy.

4. **Adjust Seasoning:** Taste the baba ganoush and add salt according to your preference. Blend again briefly to incorporate.

5. **Serve:** Transfer the baba ganoush to a serving bowl. Drizzle with extra virgin olive oil and sprinkle with chopped parsley. Optionally, garnish with pomegranate seeds or a sprinkle of sumac. Serve with pita bread, crackers, or as a dip for vegetables.

Tips for Dips and Spreads:

- **Consistency:** Adjust the consistency of hummus and baba ganoush by adding water or olive oil until they reach the desired texture.

- **Flavor Enhancement:** Experiment with additional ingredients such as roasted red peppers, sun-dried tomatoes, or fresh herbs to customize the dips to your taste.

- **Storage:** Store leftover hummus and baba ganoush in airtight containers in the refrigerator for up to one week. Stir well before serving.

Enjoy these flavorful Middle Eastern dips and spreads as appetizers, snacks, or accompaniments to meals, adding a taste of tradition and richness to your table.

11) Fresh Garden Salads

Fresh garden salads are vibrant and refreshing, incorporating a variety of crisp vegetables, herbs, and often fruits or nuts, dressed lightly to enhance their natural flavors. Here's how to create a delicious and nutritious fresh garden salad:

Ingredients:

For the Salad:

- Mixed salad greens (lettuce, spinach, arugula, etc.)
- Cherry tomatoes, halved
- Cucumber, thinly sliced
- Bell peppers, diced (red, yellow, or green)
- Red onion, thinly sliced
- Carrots, shredded or thinly sliced
- Radishes, thinly sliced
- Optional additions: avocado slices, olives, sprouts, nuts (such as almonds or walnuts),

seeds (such as sunflower or pumpkin seeds), crumbled feta cheese

For the Dressing:

- 1/4 cup extra virgin olive oil
- 2 tablespoons balsamic vinegar
- 1 teaspoon Dijon mustard
- 1 clove garlic, minced
- Salt and freshly ground black pepper, to taste

Instructions:

1. Prepare the Salad Ingredients:

- Wash and thoroughly dry the salad greens. Tear larger leaves into bite-sized pieces and place them in a large salad bowl.
- Add the cherry tomatoes, cucumber slices, diced bell peppers, thinly sliced red onion, shredded carrots, and sliced radishes to the salad bowl. Toss gently to combine.
- If using optional additions like avocado slices, olives, nuts, seeds, or feta cheese, sprinkle them over the salad.

2. Make the Dressing:

- In a small bowl or glass jar, combine the extra virgin olive oil, balsamic vinegar, Dijon mustard, minced garlic, salt, and pepper. Whisk or shake vigorously until the dressing is well combined and emulsified.

3. Assemble the Salad:

- Drizzle the dressing over the salad ingredients, starting with a small amount. Toss the salad gently to coat evenly with the dressing. Add more dressing as needed, tasting as you go to achieve the desired flavor.

- Ensure all ingredients are well combined and evenly coated with the dressing. Adjust seasoning with additional salt and pepper if necessary.

4. Serve:

- Transfer the fresh garden salad to individual serving plates or a large serving platter. Garnish with additional herbs or toppings if desired.

- Serve immediately as a light and nutritious side dish or main course. Fresh garden salads are perfect for lunch, dinner, or as a refreshing accompaniment to grilled meats or seafood.

Tips for Fresh Garden Salads:

- **Variety:** Experiment with different combinations of salad greens and vegetables based on seasonal availability and personal preference.

- **Texture:** Incorporate crunchy elements like nuts, seeds, or croutons for added texture contrast.

- **Customization:** Customize the salad with protein additions such as grilled chicken, shrimp, or tofu for a more substantial meal.

- **Preparation:** Prep salad ingredients ahead of time but dress the salad just before serving to keep it crisp and fresh.

Enjoy the vibrant colors, flavors, and nutritional benefits of this fresh garden salad, showcasing the best of seasonal produce in a simple and delightful dish.

12) *Hearty Lentil Soup*

Hearty lentil soup is a comforting and nutritious dish, packed with protein, fiber, and essential nutrients. This recipe creates a flavorful soup that is perfect for warming up on chilly days. Here's how to make a delicious hearty lentil soup:

Ingredients:

- 1 cup dried lentils (green or brown), rinsed and drained
- 1 onion, finely chopped
- 2 carrots, diced
- 2 celery stalks, diced
- 3 garlic cloves, minced
- 1 can (14 oz) diced tomatoes
- 6 cups vegetable or chicken broth
- 1 teaspoon ground cumin
- 1 teaspoon ground coriander
- 1/2 teaspoon smoked paprika (optional)
- 1 bay leaf
- Salt and freshly ground black pepper, to taste
- 2 tablespoons olive oil
- Fresh parsley or cilantro, chopped (for garnish)
- Lemon wedges (for serving)

Instructions:

1. **Sauté Aromatics:**

- Heat olive oil in a large pot or Dutch oven over medium heat. Add the chopped onion, carrots, and celery. Sauté for 5-7 minutes, or until the vegetables begin to soften.

2. **Add Garlic and Spices:**

    - Stir in the minced garlic, ground cumin, ground coriander, and smoked paprika (if using). Cook for 1 minute, stirring constantly, until fragrant.

3. **Add Lentils and Liquid:**

    - Add the rinsed lentils, diced tomatoes (with their juices), bay leaf, and vegetable or chicken broth to the pot. Stir well to combine.

4. **Simmer the Soup:**

    - Bring the soup to a boil, then reduce the heat to low. Cover and simmer for 25-30 minutes, or until the lentils are tender. Stir occasionally to prevent sticking.

5. **Season and Serve:**

    - Once the lentils are cooked through, season the soup with salt and pepper to taste. Remove the bay leaf and discard.

6. **Garnish and Serve:**

    o Ladle the hearty lentil soup into bowls. Garnish with chopped fresh parsley or cilantro. Serve hot with lemon wedges on the side for squeezing over the soup.

Tips for Making Hearty Lentil Soup:

- **Variations:** Add diced potatoes, spinach, or kale for extra texture and nutrition.

- **Texture:** For a smoother soup, blend a portion of the soup with an immersion blender before serving.

- **Storage:** Store leftover soup in an airtight container in the refrigerator for up to 4 days, or freeze for longer storage. Reheat gently on the stovetop or in the microwave.

This hearty lentil soup is not only satisfying and comforting but also a wholesome meal that can be enjoyed as a main course or a hearty starter. It's perfect for cozy dinners and makes excellent leftovers for lunch the next day.

13) Chilled Gazpacho

Chilled gazpacho is a refreshing and flavorful Spanish soup that is perfect for hot summer days. It features ripe tomatoes and other fresh vegetables blended together with herbs and seasonings. Here's how to make a delicious chilled gazpacho:

Ingredients:

- 6 ripe tomatoes, cored and roughly chopped
- 1 cucumber, peeled and roughly chopped
- 1 red bell pepper, seeded and roughly chopped
- 1 small red onion, roughly chopped
- 2 cloves garlic, minced
- 1/4 cup extra virgin olive oil
- 2 tablespoons vinegar
- 1 teaspoon salt, or to taste
- 1/2 teaspoon freshly ground black pepper
- 1/2 teaspoon ground cumin
- Dash of hot sauce (optional)
- 1 cup tomato juice or vegetable broth (if needed for consistency)
- Fresh basil or parsley, chopped (for garnish)
- Croutons or diced avocado (optional, for garnish)

Instructions:

1. **Prepare Vegetables:**
   - In a blender or food processor, combine the chopped tomatoes, cucumber, red bell pepper, red onion, and minced garlic.

2. **Blend Ingredients:**
   - Blend the vegetables until smooth. You may need to work in batches depending on the size of your blender or food processor.

3. **Season and Chill:**
   - Add the extra virgin olive oil, vinegar, salt, black pepper, ground cumin, and hot sauce (if using) to the blended vegetables. Blend again until well combined.

4. **Adjust Consistency:**
   - If the gazpacho is too thick, add tomato juice or vegetable broth, a little at a time, until you reach your desired consistency. Blend briefly after each addition.

5. **Chill the Gazpacho:**

- Transfer the gazpacho to a large bowl or container. Cover and refrigerate for at least 2 hours, or until thoroughly chilled.

6. **Serve:**
   - Stir the chilled gazpacho before serving. Ladle into bowls and garnish with chopped fresh basil or parsley. Add croutons or diced avocado on top if desired.

Tips for Making Chilled Gazpacho:

- **Tomatoes:** Use ripe, flavorful tomatoes for the best taste. If fresh tomatoes are not available, you can use canned tomatoes, drained.

- **Texture:** For a chunkier gazpacho, reserve some of the chopped vegetables before blending and stir them into the soup before serving.

- **Flavor Enhancement:** Adjust the seasonings according to your taste preferences. Gazpacho should be tangy and well-seasoned.

Chilled gazpacho is a light and refreshing soup that showcases the fresh flavors of summer vegetables. Enjoy it as a starter or a light meal, accompanied by crusty bread or a side salad for a delightful summer dining experience.

PART 4: MAIN COURSES

Explore a diverse selection of main courses that showcase the versatility of culinary creativity. From perfectly roasted chicken and aromatic curries to succulent grilled seafood and hearty vegetarian options, this section offers something for every taste preference and dietary need.

14) Perfectly Roasted Chicken

Roasting a whole chicken to perfection results in juicy, flavorful meat with crispy skin. Here's how to make a classic roasted chicken that's tender and delicious:

Ingredients:

- 1 whole chicken (about 4-5 pounds)
- 2-3 tablespoons olive oil or melted butter
- Salt and freshly ground black pepper
- 1 lemon, halved
- Fresh herbs (such as thyme, rosemary, or sage)
- Optional: garlic cloves, peeled

Instructions:

1. **Preparation:**
    - Preheat your oven to 425°F (220°C). Remove the chicken from the refrigerator and let it sit at room temperature for about 30 minutes before roasting.

2. **Seasoning:**
    - Pat the chicken dry with paper towels. Drizzle olive oil or brush melted butter all over the chicken, making sure to coat it

evenly. Season generously inside and out with salt and freshly ground black pepper.

- Stuff the cavity of the chicken with halved lemon, fresh herbs (such as thyme, rosemary, or sage), and optional garlic cloves for extra flavor.

3. **Trussing (Optional):**

    - Truss the chicken by tying the legs together with kitchen twine. This helps the chicken cook evenly and keeps its shape.

4. **Roasting:**

    - Place the chicken breast side up on a roasting pan or a baking dish with a rack. Tuck the wing tips under the body of the chicken to prevent burning.

    - Roast the chicken in the preheated oven for about 1 hour to 1 hour 15 minutes, or until the internal temperature reaches 165°F (75°C) in the thickest part of the thigh without touching the bone.

5. **Resting:**

    - Once cooked, remove the chicken from the oven and let it rest for 10-15 minutes before carving. This allows the juices to redistribute throughout the meat, ensuring a moist and tender chicken.

6. **Carving:**
    - Carve the roasted chicken into serving pieces. Serve with pan juices or your favorite gravy alongside roasted vegetables, potatoes, or a fresh salad.

Tips for Perfectly Roasted Chicken:

- **Temperature:** Use a meat thermometer to ensure the chicken is cooked to the correct temperature. Insert the thermometer into the thickest part of the thigh without touching the bone.

- **Crispy Skin:** For extra crispy skin, you can start roasting the chicken at a higher temperature (around 450°F / 230°C) for the first 15 minutes, then reduce the temperature to 425°F / 220°C for the remaining cooking time.

- **Flavor Variations:** Experiment with different herb and seasoning combinations, such as garlic powder, paprika, or dried herbs, to suit your taste preferences.

Roasting a whole chicken is a classic cooking technique that yields a comforting and delicious meal. Mastering this method allows you to enjoy tender, juicy chicken with minimal effort, making it perfect for family dinners or special occasions.

15) Chicken Curry

Chicken curry is a popular and comforting dish enjoyed in various forms across different cultures. This recipe offers a flavorful and aromatic curry that pairs well with rice or bread. Here's how to make a delicious chicken curry:

Ingredients:

- 1.5 lbs (about 700g) boneless, skinless chicken thighs or breasts, cut into bite-sized pieces
- 2 tablespoons vegetable oil or ghee
- 1 large onion, finely chopped
- 3 cloves garlic, minced
- 1-inch piece of ginger, grated or minced
- 2 tomatoes, chopped
- 1 teaspoon ground cumin
- 1 teaspoon ground coriander
- 1/2 teaspoon turmeric powder
- 1/2 teaspoon chili powder (adjust to taste)

- 1/2 teaspoon paprika (optional, for color)
- 1/2 teaspoon garam masala
- 1/4 teaspoon ground cinnamon
- Salt, to taste
- Freshly ground black pepper, to taste
- 1 cup coconut milk (or yogurt for a different variation)
- Fresh cilantro, chopped (for garnish)
- Cooked rice or naan bread, for serving

Instructions:

1. **Sauté Aromatics:**
   - Heat vegetable oil or ghee in a large skillet or Dutch oven over medium heat. Add finely chopped onion and sauté until softened and translucent, about 5-6 minutes.

2. **Add Garlic, Ginger, and Spices:**
   - Stir in minced garlic and grated/minced ginger. Sauté for another 1-2 minutes until fragrant.

- Add ground cumin, ground coriander, turmeric powder, chili powder, paprika (if using), garam masala, ground cinnamon, salt, and black pepper. Cook for 1 minute, stirring constantly to toast the spices.

3. **Cook Chicken:**

    - Add the bite-sized chicken pieces to the skillet. Cook for 5-7 minutes, stirring occasionally, until the chicken is lightly browned on all sides.

4. **Simmer with Tomatoes:**

    - Add chopped tomatoes to the skillet. Stir to combine and cook for 3-4 minutes until the tomatoes begin to break down and release their juices.

5. **Add Coconut Milk:**

    - Pour in coconut milk (or yogurt if using) and stir well to combine. Bring the mixture to a simmer.

6. **Simmer Until Chicken is Tender:**

    - Reduce the heat to low and cover the skillet. Let the curry simmer gently for 20-25 minutes, stirring occasionally, until the chicken is cooked through and tender.

Adjust the seasoning with salt and pepper if needed.

7. **Serve:**

    o Garnish the chicken curry with freshly chopped cilantro. Serve hot over cooked rice or with naan bread on the side.

Tips for Making Chicken Curry:

- **Variations:** Feel free to customize your chicken curry by adding vegetables like potatoes, bell peppers, or peas.

- **Spice Level:** Adjust the amount of chili powder or omit it entirely based on your preference for spiciness.

- **Storage:** Chicken curry tastes even better the next day as flavors develop. Store leftovers in an airtight container in the refrigerator for up to 3 days or freeze for longer storage.

Chicken curry is a comforting and versatile dish that's perfect for weeknight dinners or special occasions. Enjoy the rich flavors and aroma of this homemade curry served with your favorite sides!

16) Grilled Chicken Kebabs

Grilled chicken kebabs are a delightful dish perfect for outdoor grilling sessions or casual dinners. This recipe emphasizes juicy chicken pieces infused with flavorful marinade and grilled to perfection. Here's how to prepare delicious grilled chicken kebabs:

Ingredients:

- 1.5 lbs (about 700g) boneless, skinless chicken breasts or thighs, cut into 1-inch cubes
- 1/4 cup olive oil
- 3 tablespoons soy sauce
- 2 tablespoons honey
- 2 cloves garlic, minced
- 1 teaspoon paprika
- 1 teaspoon ground cumin
- 1/2 teaspoon ground black pepper
- Juice of 1 lemon
- Salt, to taste
- Wooden or metal skewers

Instructions:

1. **Prepare the Marinade:**

In a bowl, combine olive oil, soy sauce, honey, minced garlic, paprika, ground cumin, black pepper, lemon juice, and a pinch of salt. Mix well to incorporate all ingredients.

2. **Marinate the Chicken:**

Place the chicken cubes in a shallow dish or resealable plastic bag. Pour the marinade over the chicken, ensuring all pieces are evenly coated. Cover the dish or seal the bag, then refrigerate for at least 1 hour to allow flavors to meld (marinating longer enhances the taste).

3. **Preheat the Grill:**

Preheat your grill to medium-high heat (around 400-450°F / 200-230°C). If using wooden skewers, soak them in water for at least 30 minutes to prevent burning.

4. **Assemble the Kebabs:**

Thread the marinated chicken pieces onto skewers, leaving a small space between each piece. If desired, alternate with chunks of bell peppers, onions, or other vegetables for added flavor and variety.

5. **Grill the Kebabs:**

Place the chicken kebabs on the preheated grill. Grill for about 10-12 minutes, turning occasionally, until the chicken is fully cooked and has nice grill marks on all sides. Baste with any remaining marinade during grilling for extra flavor and moisture.

6. **Serve:**

Once cooked through (internal temperature should reach 165°F / 75°C), remove the chicken kebabs from the grill. Let them rest for a few minutes before serving.

7. **Enjoy:**

Garnish with fresh herbs like parsley or cilantro if desired. Serve hot with rice, couscous, or a fresh salad on the side.

Tips for Grilled Chicken Kebabs:

- **Uniform Size:** Cut chicken into uniform pieces to ensure even cooking.

- **Vegetable Variations:** Experiment with different vegetables on the skewers for added flavor and color.

- **Grilling Time:** Adjust grilling time based on the size of the chicken pieces and the heat of your grill to prevent overcooking.

Grilled chicken kebabs are versatile and delicious, making them a fantastic choice for gatherings or everyday meals. Enjoy the smoky flavor and tender texture of these grilled treats straight from the barbecue!

17) Pan-Fried Steaks

Pan-frying steaks is a classic cooking method that results in tender, juicy meat with a flavorful seared crust. Here's how to achieve perfectly pan-fried steaks:

Ingredients:

- 2 boneless steaks (such as ribeye, sirloin, or strip loin), about 1-inch thick
- Salt and freshly ground black pepper, to taste
- 2 tablespoons vegetable oil or clarified butter (ghee)
- Optional: garlic cloves, fresh herbs (such as thyme or rosemary), for additional flavor

Instructions:

1. **Prepare the Steaks:**
    - Remove the steaks from the refrigerator and let them come to room temperature for about 30 minutes. Pat them dry with paper towels to ensure even browning.

2. **Season the Steaks:**
    - Season both sides of the steaks generously with salt and freshly ground black pepper. You can also add minced garlic or fresh herbs for extra flavor,

pressing them gently into the surface of the meat.

3. **Preheat the Pan:**
   - Heat a heavy-bottomed skillet or cast-iron pan over medium-high heat. Add vegetable oil or clarified butter (ghee) and heat until it shimmers but does not smoke. The pan should be hot to ensure a good sear.

4. **Sear the Steaks:**
   - Carefully place the steaks in the hot pan. Cook without moving them for 3-4 minutes on the first side, depending on the desired doneness and thickness of the steaks. Avoid overcrowding the pan; cook one or two steaks at a time if necessary.

5. **Flip and Cook:**
   - Flip the steaks using tongs or a spatula. Cook for an additional 3-4 minutes on the second side for medium-rare, adjusting the time based on your preferred level of doneness (use a meat thermometer for accuracy: 130°F / 54°C for medium-rare, 140°F / 60°C for medium, 150°F / 66°C for medium-well).

6. **Rest the Steaks:**

- Remove the steaks from the pan and transfer them to a plate or cutting board. Tent loosely with foil and let them rest for 5-10 minutes. This allows the juices to redistribute within the meat for maximum tenderness.

7. **Serve:**
    - Slice the pan-fried steaks against the grain into thick slices. Serve immediately with your favorite sides, such as roasted vegetables, mashed potatoes, or a crisp salad.

Tips for Pan-Frying Steaks:

- **Pan Temperature:** Ensure the pan is hot before adding the steaks to achieve a good sear and caramelization.

- **Thickness Matters:** Adjust cooking time based on the thickness of your steaks. Thicker cuts will require longer cooking times.

- **Resting Time:** Letting the steaks rest after cooking is crucial for a juicy and flavorful result. Avoid cutting into them immediately to retain their juices.

Pan-fried steaks are a simple yet delicious way to enjoy a restaurant-quality meal at home. Mastering this cooking technique allows you to create tender, flavorful steaks tailored to your preference.

18) Slow-Cooked Beef Stew

Slow-cooked beef stew is a comforting and hearty dish, perfect for chilly days or when you crave a satisfying meal. This recipe combines tender beef, flavorful vegetables, and a rich broth that cooks slowly to perfection. Here's how to make a delicious slow-cooked beef stew:

Ingredients:

- 2 lbs (about 900g) beef stew meat, cut into bite-sized pieces
- 2 tablespoons vegetable oil
- 1 large onion, diced
- 3 cloves garlic, minced
- 3 medium carrots, peeled and sliced
- 2 celery stalks, sliced
- 1 lb (about 450g) potatoes, peeled and cut into chunks
- 1 cup beef broth
- 2 tablespoons tomato paste

- 2 bay leaves
- 1 teaspoon dried thyme
- 1 teaspoon dried rosemary
- Salt and freshly ground black pepper, to taste
- Chopped fresh parsley, for garnish

Instructions:

1. **Brown the Beef:**
   - Heat vegetable oil in a large skillet or Dutch oven over medium-high heat. Add the beef stew meat in batches, ensuring not to overcrowd the pan, and brown on all sides. This step adds flavor to the stew. Transfer browned beef to a plate.

2. **Sauté Aromatics:**
   - In the same skillet or Dutch oven, add diced onion and sauté for 3-4 minutes until softened. Add minced garlic and sauté for another minute until fragrant.

3. **Combine Ingredients:**
   - Return the browned beef to the skillet. Add sliced carrots, celery, and potatoes. Stir in beef broth, tomato paste, bay

leaves, dried thyme, and dried rosemary. Season with salt and pepper to taste.

4. **Slow Cook the Stew:**
   - Cover the skillet or transfer everything to a slow cooker if using. Cook on low heat for 6-8 hours, or until the beef and vegetables are tender and flavors have melded together. If using a slow cooker, set it to low heat and cook for the same duration.

5. **Serve:**
   - Once cooked, discard bay leaves. Taste and adjust seasoning if needed. Ladle the slow-cooked beef stew into bowls. Garnish with chopped fresh parsley for added freshness.

6. **Enjoy:**
   - Serve the beef stew hot with crusty bread or over cooked rice or mashed potatoes for a complete meal. Enjoy the comforting flavors and tender texture of this slow-cooked dish.

Tips for Making Slow-Cooked Beef Stew:

- **Cutting Meat:** Ensure the beef stew meat is cut into uniform bite-sized pieces for even cooking.

- **Vegetable Variations:** Feel free to add other vegetables like parsnips, turnips, or peas to customize the stew to your liking.

- **Thickening Sauce:** If you prefer a thicker stew, mix 2 tablespoons of cornstarch with 1/4 cup of cold water and stir it into the stew during the last hour of cooking.

Slow-cooked beef stew is a hearty and comforting meal that brings warmth to any table. Prepare this dish ahead of time for a convenient and delicious dinner option.

19) Lamb Tagine

Lamb tagine is a traditional Moroccan dish known for its tender meat, aromatic spices, and delightful combination of sweet and savory flavors. This recipe brings together succulent lamb with a blend of spices and dried fruits, slow-cooked to perfection. Here's how to make a delicious lamb tagine:

Ingredients:

- 2 lbs (about 900g) lamb shoulder or leg, cut into chunks

- 2 tablespoons olive oil

- 1 large onion, finely chopped

- 3 cloves garlic, minced

- 1 teaspoon ground cumin
- 1 teaspoon ground coriander
- 1 teaspoon ground cinnamon
- 1/2 teaspoon ground ginger
- 1/2 teaspoon ground turmeric
- 1/4 teaspoon ground cloves
- Pinch of saffron threads (optional, for added flavor)
- Salt and freshly ground black pepper, to taste
- 1 cup beef or lamb broth
- 1/2 cup dried apricots, chopped
- 1/2 cup dried prunes, chopped
- Zest of 1 lemon
- 2 tablespoons honey
- Fresh cilantro or parsley, chopped, for garnish
- Cooked couscous or rice, for serving

Instructions:

1. **Brown the Lamb:**

- Heat olive oil in a large skillet or tagine pot over medium-high heat. Add the lamb chunks in batches and brown them on all sides. This step enhances the flavor of the dish. Transfer browned lamb to a plate.

2. **Sauté Aromatics:**

    - In the same skillet or tagine pot, add chopped onion and sauté for 5-6 minutes until softened and translucent. Add minced garlic and sauté for another minute until fragrant.

3. **Add Spices and Broth:**

    - Return the browned lamb to the skillet or tagine pot. Add ground cumin, ground coriander, ground cinnamon, ground ginger, ground turmeric, ground cloves, saffron threads (if using), salt, and black pepper. Stir well to coat the lamb with spices.

    - Pour in beef or lamb broth, scraping the bottom of the pot to deglaze and incorporate any browned bits. Bring to a simmer.

4. **Slow Cook the Tagine:**

    - Cover the skillet or tagine pot with a lid and reduce the heat to low. Let the lamb tagine simmer gently for 1.5 to 2 hours, or until the lamb is tender and cooked through. Stir occasionally and add more broth if needed to maintain moisture.

5. **Add Dried Fruits and Honey:**

    o Stir in chopped dried apricots, dried prunes, lemon zest, and honey. Simmer for an additional 15-20 minutes, or until the fruits are softened and the flavors have melded together.

6. **Serve:**

    o Taste and adjust seasoning if needed. Garnish the lamb tagine with chopped fresh cilantro or parsley. Serve hot over cooked couscous or rice.

Tips for Making Lamb Tagine:

- **Tagine Pot:** If using a traditional tagine pot, ensure to soak it in water for 1 hour before use to prevent cracking when placed on direct heat.

- **Dried Fruits:** Experiment with different combinations of dried fruits like figs, dates, or raisins to vary the flavors of your tagine.

- **Slow Cooking:** Slow cooking is key to achieving tender and flavorful lamb. Allow enough time for the meat to simmer and absorb the spices and broth.

Lamb tagine is a delightful dish that brings the exotic flavors of Morocco to your table. Enjoy the aromatic spices, tender lamb, and sweet dried fruits in this comforting and satisfying meal.

20) Grilled Fish Fillets

Grilled fish fillets are a light and flavorful dish that's perfect for a healthy meal option. This recipe focuses on simple preparation and grilling techniques to bring out the natural flavors of the fish. Here's how to make delicious grilled fish fillets:

Ingredients:

- 4 fish fillets (such as salmon, tilapia, trout, or any firm white fish), about 6 oz (170g) each
- 2 tablespoons olive oil
- Juice of 1 lemon
- 2 cloves garlic, minced
- 1 teaspoon paprika
- 1/2 teaspoon ground cumin
- 1/2 teaspoon ground coriander

- Salt and freshly ground black pepper, to taste
- Fresh herbs (such as parsley, dill, or cilantro), chopped, for garnish
- Lemon wedges, for serving

Instructions:

1. **Prepare the Marinade:**
   - In a small bowl, whisk together olive oil, lemon juice, minced garlic, paprika, ground cumin, ground coriander, salt, and black pepper.

2. **Marinate the Fish:**
   - Place the fish fillets in a shallow dish or resealable plastic bag. Pour the marinade over the fish, ensuring each fillet is well coated. Cover the dish or seal the bag, then refrigerate for at least 30 minutes to allow flavors to meld.

3. **Preheat the Grill:**
   - Preheat your grill to medium-high heat (around 400-450°F / 200-230°C). Brush the grill grates with oil to prevent sticking.

4. **Grill the Fish:**

- Remove the fish fillets from the marinade and shake off excess marinade. Place the fillets directly on the preheated grill. Grill for about 3-4 minutes per side, depending on the thickness of the fillets, or until fish is opaque and flakes easily with a fork.

5. **Serve:**
    - Transfer the grilled fish fillets to a serving platter. Garnish with chopped fresh herbs and serve hot with lemon wedges on the side.

Tips for Grilling Fish Fillets:

- **Fish Selection:** Choose firm fish fillets that hold up well to grilling, such as salmon, tilapia, trout, or halibut.

- **Grill Preparation:** Ensure your grill grates are clean and well-oiled before grilling to prevent the fish from sticking.

- **Cooking Time:** Adjust grilling time based on the thickness of the fillets. Thinner fillets will cook faster than thicker ones.

Grilled fish fillets are a healthy and delicious option for quick meals or outdoor gatherings. Enjoy the natural flavors of the fish enhanced by the marinade and grilling process, complemented by fresh herbs and lemon.

21) Shrimp Stir-Fry

Shrimp stir-fry is a quick and flavorful dish that combines tender shrimp with fresh vegetables and a savory sauce. This recipe is perfect for busy weeknights when you want a nutritious meal on the table in no time. Here's how to make a delicious shrimp stir-fry:

Ingredients:

- 1 lb (about 450g) medium shrimp, peeled and deveined
- 2 tablespoons soy sauce
- 1 tablespoon oyster sauce
- 1 tablespoon hoisin sauce
- 1 tablespoon rice vinegar
- 1 teaspoon sesame oil
- 2 tablespoons vegetable oil, divided
- 3 cloves garlic, minced
- 1-inch piece of ginger, peeled and minced
- 1 red bell pepper, thinly sliced
- 1 yellow bell pepper, thinly sliced
- 1 cup snow peas, trimmed

- 1 medium carrot, thinly sliced
- Salt and freshly ground black pepper, to taste
- Cooked rice or noodles, for serving
- Chopped green onions and sesame seeds, for garnish

Instructions:

1. **Marinate the Shrimp:**
   - In a bowl, combine shrimp with soy sauce and let it marinate for about 10-15 minutes while preparing other ingredients.

2. **Prepare the Sauce:**
   - In a small bowl, whisk together oyster sauce, hoisin sauce, rice vinegar, and sesame oil. Set aside.

3. **Heat the Pan:**
   - Heat 1 tablespoon of vegetable oil in a large skillet or wok over medium-high heat.

4. **Cook the Shrimp:**
   - Add marinated shrimp to the skillet in a single layer. Cook for 2-3 minutes on each

side until shrimp turns pink and opaque. Remove shrimp from the skillet and set aside.

5. **Stir-Fry Vegetables:**

   - In the same skillet, heat the remaining 1 tablespoon of vegetable oil. Add minced garlic and ginger, and stir-fry for about 30 seconds until fragrant.

   - Add sliced bell peppers, snow peas, and carrot to the skillet. Stir-fry for 3-4 minutes until vegetables are tender-crisp.

6. **Combine Everything:**

   - Return cooked shrimp to the skillet. Pour the prepared sauce over the shrimp and vegetables. Stir well to coat everything evenly with the sauce. Cook for another 1-2 minutes until heated through.

7. **Serve:**

   - Serve the shrimp stir-fry hot over cooked rice or noodles. Garnish with chopped green onions and sesame seeds for added flavor and texture.

Tips for Making Shrimp Stir-Fry:

- **Preparation:** Have all ingredients prepped and ready before starting to stir-fry, as the cooking process is quick.

- **Sauce Adjustment:** Adjust the amount of sauce according to your preference. Add more soy sauce for saltiness or hoisin sauce for sweetness.

- **Variations:** Feel free to add other vegetables like broccoli, snap peas, or mushrooms to customize your stir-fry.

Shrimp stir-fry is a versatile dish that can be easily adapted with different vegetables and sauces. Enjoy this quick and delicious meal packed with flavors and nutrients!

22) Baked Salmon

Baked salmon is a classic dish that highlights the natural flavors of salmon with simple seasonings and gentle cooking. This recipe ensures moist and tender salmon fillets with a hint of herbs and citrus. Here's how to prepare delicious baked salmon:

Ingredients:

- 4 salmon fillets, about 6 oz (170g) each
- 2 tablespoons olive oil
- 2 tablespoons fresh lemon juice

- 2 cloves garlic, minced
- 1 teaspoon dried dill (or 1 tablespoon fresh dill, chopped)
- 1/2 teaspoon paprika
- Salt and freshly ground black pepper, to taste
- Lemon slices, for garnish
- Fresh dill or parsley, chopped, for garnish

Instructions:

1. **Preheat the Oven:**
   - Preheat your oven to 375°F (190°C). Line a baking sheet with parchment paper or lightly grease it with oil.

2. **Prepare the Salmon:**
   - Place the salmon fillets on the prepared baking sheet. Pat dry with paper towels to remove excess moisture.

3. **Make the Marinade:**
   - In a small bowl, whisk together olive oil, lemon juice, minced garlic, dried dill, paprika, salt, and black pepper.

4. **Coat the Salmon:**

- Brush the marinade over the salmon fillets, coating them evenly on all sides. Allow the salmon to marinate for about 10-15 minutes to enhance the flavors.

5. **Bake the Salmon:**

    - Bake the salmon in the preheated oven for 12-15 minutes, depending on the thickness of the fillets, or until the salmon is cooked through and flakes easily with a fork.

6. **Serve:**

    - Remove the baked salmon from the oven. Garnish with lemon slices and chopped fresh dill or parsley.

7. **Enjoy:**

    - Serve the baked salmon hot with your favorite side dishes, such as steamed vegetables, rice, or salad.

Tips for Baked Salmon:

- **Salmon Selection:** Choose fresh salmon fillets with firm, moist flesh for best results.

- **Cooking Time:** Adjust baking time based on the thickness of the salmon fillets. Thicker fillets may require slightly longer cooking.

- **Variations:** Customize the marinade with herbs like thyme or rosemary, or add a touch of honey or mustard for additional flavor.

Baked salmon is a nutritious and delicious dish that is easy to prepare for a quick weeknight dinner or a special occasion. Enjoy the tender, flaky texture and delicate flavors of this simple yet satisfying meal!

23) Stuffed Bell Peppers

Stuffed bell peppers are a versatile and satisfying dish that combines tender bell peppers with a flavorful filling of meat, rice, vegetables, and cheese. This recipe focuses on a classic preparation that can be adapted with various ingredients to suit your taste. Here's how to make delicious stuffed bell peppers:

Ingredients:

- 4 large bell peppers (any color), tops cut off and seeds removed
- 1 tablespoon olive oil
- 1 small onion, finely chopped
- 2 cloves garlic, minced
- 1 lb (about 450g) ground beef or turkey
- 1 cup cooked rice (white or brown)

- 1 can (14 oz / 400g) diced tomatoes, drained
- 1 cup shredded cheese (such as cheddar, mozzarella, or Monterey Jack), divided
- 1 teaspoon dried oregano
- 1 teaspoon dried basil
- Salt and freshly ground black pepper, to taste
- Fresh parsley or cilantro, chopped, for garnish

Instructions:

1. **Preheat the Oven:**
    - Preheat your oven to 375°F (190°C). Prepare a baking dish by lightly greasing it with oil or non-stick cooking spray.

2. **Prepare the Bell Peppers:**
    - Cut the tops off the bell peppers and remove the seeds and membranes from inside. Rinse the peppers under cold water and pat dry with paper towels.

3. **Prepare the Filling:**
    - In a large skillet, heat olive oil over medium heat. Add chopped onion and sauté for 3-4 minutes until softened. Add

minced garlic and sauté for another minute until fragrant.

- Add ground beef or turkey to the skillet. Cook, breaking up the meat with a spoon, until browned and cooked through.

4. **Combine Ingredients:**

    - Stir in cooked rice, diced tomatoes, 1/2 cup shredded cheese, dried oregano, dried basil, salt, and black pepper. Cook for another 2-3 minutes to heat through and allow flavors to meld. Remove from heat.

5. **Stuff the Bell Peppers:**

    - Spoon the filling mixture evenly into the hollowed-out bell peppers, pressing gently to pack the filling.

6. **Bake the Stuffed Peppers:**

    - Place the stuffed bell peppers upright in the prepared baking dish. Cover the dish with aluminum foil and bake in the preheated oven for 30-35 minutes, or until the peppers are tender.

7. **Add Cheese and Serve:**

- Remove the foil and sprinkle the remaining 1/2 cup of shredded cheese over the tops of the stuffed peppers. Return to the oven and bake uncovered for an additional 5-10 minutes, or until the cheese is melted and bubbly.

8. **Garnish and Serve:**
    - Remove the stuffed bell peppers from the oven. Garnish with chopped fresh parsley or cilantro. Serve hot as a main dish with a side salad or crusty bread.

Tips for Making Stuffed Bell Peppers:

- **Pepper Selection:** Choose large, firm bell peppers with flat bottoms that can stand upright in the baking dish.

- **Filling Variations:** Experiment with different fillings such as quinoa instead of rice, or add beans and corn for a vegetarian version.

- **Make-Ahead:** Stuffed bell peppers can be assembled ahead of time and stored in the refrigerator, covered, until ready to bake.

Stuffed bell peppers are a hearty and satisfying meal that combines the sweetness of bell peppers with a flavorful filling. Enjoy this classic dish for a comforting dinner option that's sure to please everyone at the table!

24) Chickpea and Spinach Curry

Chickpea and spinach curry, also known as chana saag, is a nutritious and flavorful vegetarian dish that combines chickpeas (garbanzo beans) with fresh spinach in a spiced tomato-based sauce. This recipe brings together aromatic spices and hearty ingredients for a satisfying meal. Here's how to make a delicious chickpea and spinach curry:

Ingredients:

- 1 tablespoon vegetable oil
- 1 onion, finely chopped
- 3 cloves garlic, minced
- 1-inch piece of ginger, grated
- 1 green chili, finely chopped (optional, adjust to taste)
- 1 teaspoon cumin seeds
- 1 teaspoon ground coriander
- 1/2 teaspoon turmeric powder
- 1/2 teaspoon paprika or chili powder (adjust to taste)
- 1/2 teaspoon garam masala

- 1/4 teaspoon ground cinnamon
- Salt, to taste
- 1 can (15 oz / 400g) chickpeas, drained and rinsed (or about 1.5 cups cooked chickpeas)
- 2 cups fresh spinach leaves, chopped
- 1 cup canned diced tomatoes (or 2 medium tomatoes, finely chopped)
- 1/2 cup coconut milk or cream (optional, for creamier texture)
- Fresh cilantro leaves, chopped, for garnish
- Cooked rice or naan bread, for serving

Instructions:

1. **Heat Oil and Sauté Aromatics:**
    - Heat vegetable oil in a large skillet or pot over medium heat. Add cumin seeds and cook for about 30 seconds until fragrant.
    - Add finely chopped onion and sauté for 3-4 minutes until softened and translucent.

2. **Add Spices and Aromatics:**

- Add minced garlic, grated ginger, and chopped green chili (if using). Sauté for another 1-2 minutes until aromatic.

3. **Spice Blend:**
    - Stir in ground coriander, turmeric powder, paprika or chili powder, garam masala, ground cinnamon, and salt. Cook the spices with the onion mixture for about 1 minute to toast them and release their flavors.

4. **Cook Chickpeas and Spinach:**
    - Add drained and rinsed chickpeas to the skillet. Stir well to coat them in the spice mixture.
    - Add chopped spinach leaves and canned diced tomatoes (or fresh tomatoes). Stir to combine all ingredients thoroughly.

5. **Simmer:**
    - Reduce heat to medium-low and let the curry simmer uncovered for 10-15 minutes, stirring occasionally. This allows the flavors to meld together and the sauce to thicken slightly.

6. **Add Coconut Milk (Optional):**

- For a creamier texture, stir in coconut milk or cream. Simmer for another 2-3 minutes until heated through.

7. **Adjust Seasoning and Serve:**

    - Taste and adjust salt and spices according to your preference. If the curry is too thick, add a splash of water or vegetable broth to reach your desired consistency.

8. **Garnish and Serve:**

    - Remove from heat and garnish with chopped fresh cilantro leaves. Serve hot over cooked rice or with naan bread on the side.

Tips for Making Chickpea and Spinach Curry:

- **Spice Level:** Adjust the amount of green chili and chili powder to suit your taste preferences for spiciness.

- **Creaminess:** Coconut milk or cream adds richness to the curry, but you can omit it for a lighter version.

- **Variations:** Add other vegetables like diced bell peppers or carrots for additional texture and flavor.

Chickpea and spinach curry is a comforting and nutritious dish that's perfect for vegetarians and meat-lovers alike. Enjoy the blend of spices and textures in this flavorful curry served with rice or naan for a complete meal.

25) Grilled Vegetable Platter

A grilled vegetable platter is a delightful dish that showcases the natural flavors of seasonal vegetables with a hint of smokiness from the grill. This recipe combines a variety of vegetables, seasoned simply with herbs and olive oil, for a healthy and delicious side or main dish. Here's how to prepare a grilled vegetable platter:

Ingredients:

- 1 medium eggplant, sliced into rounds
- 2 zucchini, sliced lengthwise
- 2 yellow squash, sliced lengthwise
- 1 red bell pepper, seeded and quartered
- 1 yellow bell pepper, seeded and quartered
- 1 red onion, cut into wedges
- 8-10 cherry tomatoes, on the vine
- 2 tablespoons olive oil

- 2 cloves garlic, minced
- 1 tablespoon fresh herbs (such as thyme, rosemary, or oregano), chopped
- Salt and freshly ground black pepper, to taste
- Balsamic glaze (optional), for drizzling
- Fresh basil leaves, for garnish

Instructions:

1. **Preheat the Grill:**
   - Preheat your grill to medium-high heat (around 400-450°F / 200-230°C).

2. **Prepare the Vegetables:**
   - In a large bowl, toss the sliced eggplant, zucchini, yellow squash, bell peppers, red onion, and cherry tomatoes with olive oil, minced garlic, chopped herbs, salt, and black pepper. Ensure all vegetables are evenly coated.

3. **Grill the Vegetables:**
   - Place the marinated vegetables directly on the preheated grill. Grill for about 3-4 minutes per side, or until vegetables are tender and have grill marks. Cooking

times may vary depending on the thickness of the vegetables.

4. **Assemble the Platter:**
   - Arrange the grilled vegetables on a large serving platter or wooden board. Arrange them attractively, alternating colors and shapes for visual appeal.

5. **Serve:**
   - Drizzle the grilled vegetable platter with balsamic glaze (if using) and garnish with fresh basil leaves. Serve hot as a side dish or as a main course with crusty bread or grains.

Tips for Grilled Vegetable Platter:

- **Vegetable Selection:** Use a variety of seasonal vegetables for the best flavor and texture. Other great options include asparagus, mushrooms, or artichokes.

- **Marinade Variation:** Customize the olive oil and herb marinade with your favorite spices or a squeeze of lemon juice for added freshness.

- **Presentation:** Arrange the grilled vegetables with care to create an appealing presentation. Garnish with additional herbs or a sprinkle of feta cheese for extra flavor.

Grilled vegetable platters are a versatile dish that can be served on its own, alongside grilled meats, or as part of a larger meal. Enjoy the smoky, caramelized flavors of grilled vegetables in this vibrant and nutritious dish!

PART 5: SIDE DISHES

Complement your meals with an assortment of vibrant and nutritious side dishes. From roasted root vegetables and steamed greens to fragrant rice and innovative grain salads, these recipes add depth and flavor to any dining experience, ensuring every meal is a well-rounded culinary delight.

26) Roasted Root Vegetables

Roasted root vegetables are a comforting and versatile dish that brings out the natural sweetness and earthy flavors of hearty vegetables. This recipe combines a variety of root vegetables with herbs and olive oil for a simple yet delicious side dish. Here's how to make roasted root vegetables:

Ingredients:

- 2 large carrots, peeled and cut into chunks
- 2 parsnips, peeled and cut into chunks
- 2 medium sweet potatoes, peeled and cut into chunks
- 2 medium red potatoes, cut into chunks
- 1 large red onion, cut into wedges
- 2-3 tablespoons olive oil
- 2 cloves garlic, minced
- 1 teaspoon dried thyme (or 1 tablespoon fresh thyme leaves)
- 1 teaspoon dried rosemary (or 1 tablespoon fresh rosemary, chopped)
- Salt and freshly ground black pepper, to taste

- Fresh parsley, chopped, for garnish (optional)

Instructions:

1. **Preheat the Oven:**
   - Preheat your oven to 400°F (200°C). Line a baking sheet with parchment paper or aluminum foil for easy cleanup.

2. **Prepare the Vegetables:**
   - In a large bowl, combine the chopped carrots, parsnips, sweet potatoes, red potatoes, and red onion.

3. **Season the Vegetables:**
   - Drizzle olive oil over the vegetables and add minced garlic, dried thyme, dried rosemary, salt, and black pepper. Toss well to coat all vegetables evenly with the seasoning.

4. **Roast the Vegetables:**
   - Spread the seasoned vegetables in a single layer on the prepared baking sheet.
   - Roast in the preheated oven for 30-35 minutes, stirring halfway through, until the vegetables are tender and caramelized around the edges.

5. **Serve:**
    - Remove the roasted root vegetables from the oven. Transfer to a serving dish and garnish with fresh chopped parsley, if desired.

Tips for Making Roasted Root Vegetables:

- **Vegetable Variations:** You can customize the mix of vegetables based on what you have on hand or prefer. Other options include turnips, rutabaga, beets, or butternut squash.

- **Even Cooking:** Cut the vegetables into uniform sizes to ensure even cooking. Larger chunks may require slightly longer roasting time.

- **Flavor Enhancements:** Experiment with different herbs and spices such as paprika, cumin, or a drizzle of balsamic vinegar before roasting for added flavor.

Roasted root vegetables are perfect as a side dish for roasted meats, grilled poultry, or served on their own as a hearty vegetarian option. Enjoy the rich flavors and comforting textures of this simple yet delicious dish!

Steamed Greens with Garlic

Steamed greens with garlic is a simple and nutritious dish that preserves the vibrant color and natural flavors of fresh greens. This recipe highlights the freshness of greens like spinach, kale, or Swiss chard, enhanced with aromatic garlic. Here's how to prepare steamed greens with garlic:

Ingredients:

- 1 bunch of greens (such as spinach, kale, Swiss chard, or collard greens), washed and tough stems removed
- 2 tablespoons olive oil or butter
- 2-3 cloves garlic, minced
- Salt and freshly ground black pepper, to taste
- Red pepper flakes (optional), for a hint of spice
- Lemon wedges, for serving (optional)

Instructions:

1. **Prepare the Greens:**
   - Wash the greens thoroughly under cold water. Trim off any tough stems and chop the leaves into bite-sized pieces.

2. **Steam the Greens:**
   - Fill a large pot with 1-2 inches of water and bring it to a boil over medium-high heat. Place a steamer basket inside the pot.

- Add the chopped greens to the steamer basket. Cover the pot with a lid and steam the greens for 3-5 minutes, or until they are tender and bright green.

3. **Sauté with Garlic:**

    - While the greens are steaming, heat olive oil or butter in a large skillet over medium heat. Add minced garlic and sauté for about 1 minute until fragrant, being careful not to let it brown.

4. **Combine Greens and Garlic:**

    - Transfer the steamed greens from the steamer basket to the skillet with the garlic. Toss gently to coat the greens with the garlic-infused oil.

5. **Season and Serve:**

    - Season the steamed greens with salt, black pepper, and red pepper flakes (if using), adjusting to taste.

    - Serve hot as a side dish, garnished with lemon wedges for a refreshing citrus touch if desired.

Tips for Making Steamed Greens with Garlic:

- **Greens Selection:** Use your favorite greens or a mix for variety. Spinach cooks quickly, while heartier greens like kale may require a slightly longer steaming time.

- **Flavor Variations:** Enhance the dish with a splash of soy sauce or a sprinkle of Parmesan cheese before serving for added depth of flavor.

- **Nutritional Benefits:** Steaming preserves the nutrients in greens better than boiling, making this dish a healthy addition to any meal.

Steamed greens with garlic is a quick and nutritious side dish that pairs well with grilled meats, roasted vegetables, or as part of a vegetarian meal. Enjoy the vibrant colors and fresh flavors of this simple yet satisfying dish!

27) Grilled Asparagus

Grilled asparagus is a delicious and easy-to-prepare side dish that highlights the natural sweetness and nutty flavor of asparagus while adding a hint of smokiness from the grill. Here's how to grill asparagus to perfection:

Ingredients:

- 1 bunch of asparagus spears, tough ends trimmed

- 2 tablespoons olive oil
- Salt and freshly ground black pepper, to taste
- Optional: grated Parmesan cheese, lemon wedges, or balsamic glaze for serving

Instructions:

1. **Preheat the Grill:**
   - Preheat your grill to medium-high heat. If using a gas grill, aim for around 400-450°F (200-230°C).

2. **Prepare the Asparagus:**
   - Trim the tough ends of the asparagus spears by snapping off the woody ends or cutting them with a knife if preferred.

3. **Season the Asparagus:**
   - Place the trimmed asparagus spears in a large bowl. Drizzle olive oil over the asparagus and toss to coat evenly. Season with salt and freshly ground black pepper.

4. **Grill the Asparagus:**
   - Arrange the seasoned asparagus spears in a single layer on the preheated grill grate. Grill for about 3-5 minutes, turning

occasionally, until the asparagus is tender and lightly charred.

5. **Serve:**

    - Remove the grilled asparagus from the grill and transfer to a serving platter.

    - Optionally, sprinkle grated Parmesan cheese over the hot grilled asparagus for added flavor. Serve with lemon wedges on the side for a citrusy touch or drizzle with balsamic glaze for a hint of sweetness.

Tips for Grilling Asparagus:

- **Uniform Cooking:** Choose asparagus spears that are similar in thickness for even grilling. Thicker spears may require slightly longer cooking time.

- **Grilling Basket or Foil:** To prevent smaller asparagus spears from falling through the grill grates, use a grilling basket or wrap them in foil with a few holes punched in for ventilation.

- **Variations:** Experiment with different seasonings such as garlic powder, smoked paprika, or a squeeze of fresh lemon juice before grilling for added flavor.

Grilled asparagus is a versatile side dish that pairs well with grilled meats, seafood, or served alongside salads.

Enjoy the tender-crisp texture and smoky flavor of grilled asparagus for a simple and delicious addition to any meal!

28) Perfectly Cooked Rice

Cooking rice to perfection involves a few key steps to achieve fluffy, separate grains with just the right texture. Here's a guide to cooking perfectly cooked rice, whether you're using a stovetop method or a rice cooker:

Ingredients:

- 1 cup long-grain white rice (such as basmati or jasmine)
- 1 3/4 cups water or broth (adjust according to rice variety)
- Salt, to taste (optional)

Stovetop Method:

1. **Rinse the Rice:**
    - Place the rice in a fine-mesh sieve and rinse under cold water until the water runs clear. This removes excess starch and helps prevent the rice from becoming sticky.

2. **Cooking:**
    - In a medium saucepan, combine the rinsed rice and water (or broth) with a

pinch of salt if desired. Bring to a boil over medium-high heat.

3. **Simmer:**

    o Once boiling, reduce the heat to low and cover the saucepan with a tight-fitting lid. Simmer the rice for 15-20 minutes, depending on the variety of rice used. Check the package instructions for specific cooking times.

4. **Steam:**

    o After the cooking time is complete, remove the saucepan from heat but keep the lid on. Let the rice steam for an additional 5-10 minutes. This step allows the rice to finish cooking and absorb any remaining moisture.

5. **Fluff and Serve:**

    o Remove the lid and fluff the rice gently with a fork to separate the grains. Serve immediately as a side dish or as a base for other dishes.

Rice Cooker Method:

1. **Rinse the Rice:**

- Rinse the rice as described above until the water runs clear.

2. **Measure and Add Water:**
   - Transfer the rinsed rice to the rice cooker pot. Add the appropriate amount of water or broth according to the rice cooker's instructions.

3. **Cook:**
   - Close the rice cooker lid and select the appropriate setting (usually "white rice" or similar). Start the rice cooker and let it cook according to the manufacturer's instructions.

4. **Steam:**
   - Once the rice cooker automatically switches to "keep warm" mode or signals that it's done, let the rice steam with the lid closed for an additional 5-10 minutes.

5. **Fluff and Serve:**
   - Open the rice cooker lid and fluff the rice gently with a fork to separate the grains. Serve immediately.

Tips for Perfectly Cooked Rice:

- **Water Ratio:** The ratio of rice to water can vary slightly depending on the type of rice and personal preference. Adjust the water amount accordingly for firmer or softer rice.

- **Resting Time:** Allowing the rice to steam off heat after cooking ensures even texture and fluffy grains.

- **Seasoning:** Consider adding a knob of butter, a dash of olive oil, or fresh herbs like parsley or cilantro after cooking for extra flavor.

Perfectly cooked rice serves as a versatile base for various dishes, from stir-fries to curries and pilafs. Mastering these cooking techniques ensures that you consistently achieve delicious, fluffy rice every time.

29) *Quinoa Salad*

Quinoa salad is a nutritious and flavorful dish that combines fluffy quinoa with fresh vegetables, herbs, and a zesty dressing. This recipe is versatile, allowing you to customize the ingredients based on your preferences. Here's how to make a delicious quinoa salad:

Ingredients:

- 1 cup quinoa, rinsed
- 2 cups water or vegetable broth
- 1/2 teaspoon salt

- 1 cup cherry tomatoes, halved
- 1 cucumber, diced
- 1 bell pepper (any color), diced
- 1/4 cup red onion, finely chopped
- 1/4 cup fresh parsley, chopped
- 1/4 cup fresh mint leaves, chopped (optional)
- 1/4 cup olive oil
- 2 tablespoons fresh lemon juice
- 1 clove garlic, minced
- Salt and freshly ground black pepper, to taste
- Optional add-ins: diced avocado, crumbled feta cheese, chickpeas, or grilled chicken

Instructions:

1. **Cook the Quinoa:**
    - In a medium saucepan, combine quinoa, water or broth, and salt. Bring to a boil over medium-high heat.
    - Reduce the heat to low, cover the saucepan with a lid, and simmer for 15-20 minutes, or until the quinoa is cooked and

the liquid is absorbed. Remove from heat and let it sit, covered, for 5 minutes. Fluff the quinoa with a fork and let it cool to room temperature.

2. **Prepare the Vegetables:**

    o   While the quinoa is cooking, prepare the vegetables. Dice the cherry tomatoes, cucumber, bell pepper, red onion, parsley, and mint (if using). Place them in a large mixing bowl.

3. **Make the Dressing:**

    o   In a small bowl, whisk together olive oil, lemon juice, minced garlic, salt, and black pepper to make the dressing.

4. **Assemble the Salad:**

    o   Add the cooled quinoa to the bowl of vegetables. Pour the dressing over the salad and toss gently to combine, ensuring the quinoa and vegetables are evenly coated.

5. **Chill and Serve:**

    o   Refrigerate the quinoa salad for at least 30 minutes to allow the flavors to meld together.

6. **Serve:**
    - Before serving, taste and adjust the seasoning if needed. Optionally, add diced avocado, crumbled feta cheese, chickpeas, or grilled chicken for extra protein and flavor.

7. **Garnish:**
    - Garnish with additional chopped herbs, such as parsley or mint, for freshness.

Tips for Making Quinoa Salad:

- **Quinoa:** Rinse the quinoa thoroughly before cooking to remove any bitterness from the outer coating.

- **Vegetables:** Feel free to customize the vegetables based on what you have on hand or seasonal availability.

- **Dressing:** The lemon-garlic dressing adds a bright and tangy flavor to the salad. Adjust the amount of lemon juice and olive oil to suit your taste preference.

Quinoa salad is perfect for meal prep, picnics, or as a refreshing side dish for any occasion. Enjoy the nutritious blend of quinoa and colorful vegetables with this versatile and delicious recipe!

Lentil Pilaf

Lentil pilaf is a hearty and nutritious dish that combines tender lentils with aromatic spices and fluffy rice. This recipe yields a flavorful and satisfying meal or side dish. Here's how to make lentil pilaf:

Ingredients:

- 1 cup brown or green lentils, rinsed
- 1 cup basmati rice, rinsed
- 2 tablespoons olive oil or butter
- 1 onion, finely chopped
- 2 cloves garlic, minced
- 1 teaspoon ground cumin
- 1/2 teaspoon ground coriander
- 1/2 teaspoon ground turmeric
- 1/4 teaspoon ground cinnamon
- 2 cups vegetable or chicken broth
- Salt and freshly ground black pepper, to taste
- Fresh cilantro or parsley, chopped (optional, for garnish)

Instructions:

1. **Prepare the Lentils and Rice:**
   - Rinse the lentils and rice separately under cold water until the water runs clear. Set aside.

2. **Sauté the Aromatics:**
   - Heat olive oil or butter in a large saucepan or Dutch oven over medium heat. Add chopped onion and sauté until translucent, about 5 minutes.
   - Add minced garlic, ground cumin, ground coriander, ground turmeric, and ground cinnamon. Cook, stirring constantly, for 1-2 minutes until fragrant.

3. **Cook the Lentils:**
   - Add rinsed lentils to the pan and stir to coat with the onion and spice mixture.
   - Pour in the vegetable or chicken broth and bring to a boil. Reduce the heat to low, cover the pan with a lid, and simmer for 15-20 minutes, or until the lentils are tender but still hold their shape.

4. **Add the Rice:**
   - Stir in the rinsed rice and season with salt and freshly ground black pepper.

- Bring the mixture back to a boil, then reduce the heat to low. Cover the pan with a lid and simmer for an additional 15-20 minutes, or until the rice is cooked and the liquid is absorbed.

5. **Fluff and Serve:**

    - Once the rice and lentils are cooked and tender, remove the pan from heat. Let it sit, covered, for 5-10 minutes to steam.

    - Fluff the lentil pilaf with a fork to combine the lentils and rice. Adjust seasoning with salt and pepper if needed.

6. **Garnish and Serve:**

    - Garnish the lentil pilaf with chopped fresh cilantro or parsley, if desired, for added freshness and color.

Tips for Making Lentil Pilaf:

- **Variations:** Add diced vegetables such as carrots, bell peppers, or peas during the sautéing step for extra flavor and nutrition.

- **Spices:** Adjust the spice levels according to your preference. For a spicier pilaf, add a pinch of cayenne pepper or red pepper flakes.

- **Storage:** Lentil pilaf makes excellent leftovers. Store any leftovers in an airtight container in the refrigerator for up to 3-4 days.

Lentil pilaf is a wholesome and comforting dish that can be served as a main course or alongside grilled meats or vegetables. Enjoy the rich flavors and nutritional benefits of this delicious lentil pilaf recipe!

30) Homemade Pasta

Making homemade pasta is a rewarding culinary experience that results in fresh, tender noodles perfect for various sauces and dishes. Here's a guide to making homemade pasta from scratch:

Ingredients:

- 2 cups all-purpose flour, plus extra for dusting
- 2 large eggs
- 1/2 teaspoon salt
- Water, as needed

Equipment Needed:

- Rolling pin or pasta machine
- Large clean work surface

Instructions:

1. **Prepare the Pasta Dough:**
   - On a clean work surface, mound the flour and create a well in the center. Crack the eggs into the well and add salt.
   - Using a fork, gradually whisk the eggs while incorporating the flour from the

edges of the well. Continue mixing until a dough forms.

- If the dough is too dry, add water, a tablespoon at a time, until the dough comes together. If it's too sticky, add a little more flour.

2. **Knead the Dough:**

   - Knead the dough for about 8-10 minutes until it becomes smooth, elastic, and no longer sticky. This develops gluten and ensures the pasta's texture.

3. **Rest the Dough:**

   - Wrap the dough in plastic wrap and let it rest at room temperature for at least 30 minutes. This allows the gluten to relax and makes the dough easier to roll out.

4. **Roll Out the Pasta:**

   - Divide the rested dough into smaller portions. Work with one portion at a time, keeping the rest covered to prevent drying.

   - Flatten the dough portion with your hands or a rolling pin into a rough rectangle or oval shape.

- Using a pasta machine or a rolling pin, roll the dough out gradually into thin sheets. Dust the dough with flour as needed to prevent sticking.
- Continue rolling and folding the dough through the pasta machine, adjusting to thinner settings until you achieve the desired thickness (usually setting 5-6 on most pasta machines).

5. **Shape the Pasta:**
   - Once rolled out, you can cut the pasta sheets into various shapes like fettuccine, tagliatelle, or pappardelle using a pasta machine or a sharp knife.
   - Alternatively, use a pasta machine's cutter attachment for specific shapes or hand-cut for rustic noodles.

6. **Cook the Pasta:**
   - Bring a large pot of salted water to a boil. Cook the fresh pasta for 2-4 minutes, depending on thickness, until al dente (firm to the bite).

7. **Serve:**
   - Drain the pasta and toss with your favorite sauce immediately. Homemade

pasta cooks faster than dried pasta, so keep an eye on it to avoid overcooking.

Tips for Making Homemade Pasta:

- **Flour:** Use semolina flour or a blend for a heartier texture, or experiment with whole wheat flour for added nuttiness.

- **Drying:** If not cooking immediately, hang freshly cut pasta on a pasta drying rack or lay it flat on a floured surface to dry for a few hours. Once dry, store in an airtight container for up to a week.

- **Variations:** Add herbs, spinach, or tomato paste to the dough for flavored pasta. Experiment with different shapes and sizes to suit your dish.

Making homemade pasta allows for endless creativity and ensures the freshest pasta possible for your favorite sauces and dishes. Enjoy the satisfaction of creating and savoring delicious, tender noodles with this homemade pasta recipe!

31) *Classic Spaghetti with Tomato Sauce*

Classic spaghetti with tomato sauce is a timeless and comforting dish loved for its simplicity and satisfying flavors. Here's a traditional recipe to prepare this iconic pasta dish:

Ingredients:

- 8 ounces (225g) spaghetti pasta
- 2 tablespoons olive oil
- 2 cloves garlic, minced
- 1/4 teaspoon red pepper flakes (optional, for heat)
- 1 can (14 ounces) diced tomatoes, with juices
- 1/2 teaspoon dried oregano
- 1/2 teaspoon dried basil
- Salt and freshly ground black pepper, to taste
- Fresh basil leaves, chopped, for garnish (optional)
- Grated Parmesan cheese, for serving

Instructions:

1. **Cook the Spaghetti:**
    - Bring a large pot of salted water to a boil. Add the spaghetti pasta and cook according to the package instructions until al dente, usually about 8-10 minutes. Reserve about 1/2 cup of pasta water before draining.

2. **Prepare the Sauce:**

    o While the pasta is cooking, heat olive oil in a large skillet over medium heat. Add minced garlic and red pepper flakes (if using), sauté for 1 minute until fragrant but not browned.

    o Stir in the diced tomatoes with their juices, dried oregano, and dried basil. Season with salt and freshly ground black pepper to taste.

3. **Simmer the Sauce:**

    o Bring the tomato sauce to a simmer. Reduce the heat to low and let it simmer gently for about 10 minutes, stirring occasionally, until the flavors meld together and the sauce thickens slightly.

4. **Combine Pasta and Sauce:**

    o Add the cooked spaghetti to the skillet with the tomato sauce. Toss gently to coat the pasta evenly with the sauce. If the sauce seems too thick, add a splash of reserved pasta water to loosen it.

5. **Serve:**

    o Transfer the spaghetti with tomato sauce to serving plates or bowls. Garnish with chopped fresh basil leaves and grated Parmesan cheese.

Tips for Making Classic Spaghetti with Tomato Sauce:

- **Tomatoes:** Use good-quality canned diced tomatoes for convenience and flavor. You can also use fresh tomatoes if they are in season—just blanch, peel, and dice them before cooking.

- **Fresh Herbs:** Substitute dried herbs with fresh if available. Add chopped fresh basil or parsley at the end for a burst of freshness.

- **Variations:** Enhance the sauce with additions like sautéed mushrooms, olives, or cooked ground meat for a heartier dish.

- **Storage:** Leftover spaghetti with tomato sauce can be stored in an airtight container in the refrigerator for up to 3-4 days. Reheat gently on the stovetop or in the microwave before serving.

Classic spaghetti with tomato sauce is a comforting meal that can be enjoyed on its own or paired with a crisp salad and crusty bread. Enjoy the simplicity and delicious flavors of this beloved pasta dish!

32) Stir-Fried Noodles

Stir-fried noodles are a quick and versatile dish that can be customized with various vegetables, proteins, and sauces. Here's a basic recipe to make delicious stir-fried noodles at home:

Ingredients:

- 8 ounces (225g) noodles of your choice (such as egg noodles, rice noodles, or udon noodles)
- 2 tablespoons soy sauce
- 1 tablespoon oyster sauce (optional)
- 1 tablespoon hoisin sauce (optional)
- 1 teaspoon sesame oil
- 1 tablespoon vegetable oil or peanut oil
- 2 cloves garlic, minced
- 1-inch piece of ginger, grated or minced
- 1 small onion, thinly sliced
- 1 bell pepper, thinly sliced
- 1 carrot, julienned
- 1 cup cabbage, thinly sliced
- 1 cup broccoli florets (optional)
- 1/2 cup sliced mushrooms (optional)

- 2 green onions, chopped (green parts only)
- Salt and freshly ground black pepper, to taste
- Sesame seeds and chopped cilantro or parsley, for garnish (optional)

Instructions:

1. **Cook the Noodles:**
   - Cook the noodles according to the package instructions until al dente. Drain and rinse under cold water to stop the cooking process. Toss with a little oil to prevent sticking and set aside.

2. **Prepare the Sauce:**
   - In a small bowl, whisk together soy sauce, oyster sauce (if using), hoisin sauce (if using), and sesame oil. Set aside.

3. **Stir-Fry the Vegetables:**
   - Heat vegetable oil or peanut oil in a large skillet or wok over medium-high heat. Add minced garlic and grated ginger, sauté for about 30 seconds until fragrant.
   - Add sliced onion, bell pepper, carrot, cabbage, broccoli florets (if using), and sliced mushrooms (if using). Stir-fry for 3-

4 minutes until the vegetables are tender-crisp.

4. **Combine Noodles and Sauce:**
   - Add the cooked noodles to the skillet or wok with the stir-fried vegetables. Pour the prepared sauce over the noodles and vegetables.

5. **Stir-Fry:**
   - Toss everything together using tongs or a spatula, ensuring the noodles and vegetables are evenly coated with the sauce. Stir-fry for an additional 2-3 minutes until heated through.

6. **Adjust Seasoning:**
   - Taste and adjust seasoning with salt and freshly ground black pepper if needed. If you prefer a saucier dish, you can add a little more soy sauce or a splash of water.

7. **Serve:**
   - Transfer the stir-fried noodles to serving plates or bowls. Garnish with chopped green onions, sesame seeds, and chopped cilantro or parsley if desired.

Tips for Making Stir-Fried Noodles:

- **Noodle Varieties:** Use your favorite type of noodles for stir-frying, such as egg noodles, rice noodles, or udon noodles. Adjust cooking time according to the type of noodles used.

- **Proteins:** Add cooked chicken, shrimp, tofu, or beef strips for added protein and flavor.

- **Vegetable Options:** Customize the vegetables based on what you have on hand or your preference. Other great additions include snap peas, bean sprouts, or baby corn.

- **Make it Spicy:** For a spicy kick, add sriracha sauce, chili paste, or crushed red pepper flakes to the sauce mixture.

Stir-fried noodles are a versatile and satisfying dish that can be enjoyed as a main course or as a side dish with your favorite Asian-inspired meals. Experiment with different ingredients and sauces to create your own unique stir-fried noodle recipe!

PART 6: DESSERTS

Indulge in a sweet finale with decadent desserts that are sure to satisfy any sweet tooth. From classic cakes and traditional pastries to creamy puddings and elegant tarts, these recipes combine simplicity with sophistication, making every dessert an unforgettable culinary experience.

33) Classic Chocolate Cake

A classic chocolate cake is a beloved dessert that satisfies with its rich cocoa flavor and moist texture. Here's a recipe to create a decadent chocolate cake that will delight any chocolate lover:

Ingredients:

- 1 and 3/4 cups (220g) all-purpose flour
- 1 and 1/2 cups (300g) granulated sugar
- 3/4 cup (65g) unsweetened cocoa powder
- 1 and 1/2 teaspoons baking powder
- 1 and 1/2 teaspoons baking soda
- 1 teaspoon salt
- 2 large eggs, at room temperature
- 1 cup (240ml) whole milk, at room temperature
- 1/2 cup (120ml) vegetable oil or melted butter
- 2 teaspoons vanilla extract
- 1 cup (240ml) boiling water

Chocolate Frosting:

- 1 cup (230g) unsalted butter, softened

- 3 and 1/2 cups (440g) powdered sugar
- 1/2 cup (45g) unsweetened cocoa powder
- 1/2 teaspoon salt
- 2 teaspoons vanilla extract
- 4-6 tablespoons heavy cream or milk

Instructions:

1. **Preheat the Oven:**
   - Preheat your oven to 350°F (175°C). Grease and flour two 9-inch round cake pans or line them with parchment paper.

2. **Prepare the Cake Batter:**
   - In a large mixing bowl, sift together flour, sugar, cocoa powder, baking powder, baking soda, and salt.
   - Add eggs, milk, oil (or melted butter), and vanilla extract. Beat on medium speed for 2 minutes until well combined.
   - Gradually stir in boiling water until the batter is smooth. The batter will be thin, but that's okay.

3. **Bake the Cake:**

- Pour the batter evenly into the prepared cake pans.
- Bake for 30-35 minutes, or until a toothpick inserted into the center comes out clean.
- Remove from the oven and allow the cakes to cool in the pans for 10 minutes. Then, remove from pans and transfer to wire racks to cool completely.

4. **Make the Chocolate Frosting:**
    - In a large mixing bowl, beat softened butter until creamy and smooth.
    - Gradually add powdered sugar and cocoa powder, alternating with heavy cream or milk and beating well after each addition.
    - Add vanilla extract and salt, beating until smooth and fluffy. If the frosting is too thick, add more cream or milk, a tablespoon at a time, until desired consistency is reached.

5. **Assemble the Cake:**
    - Once the cakes are completely cooled, place one cake layer on a serving plate or cake stand.

- Spread a layer of chocolate frosting evenly over the top of the first cake layer.
- Place the second cake layer on top and frost the top and sides of the cake with the remaining chocolate frosting.

6. **Decorate and Serve:**
    - Decorate the cake with chocolate shavings, sprinkles, or additional decorations if desired.
    - Slice and serve this delicious classic chocolate cake to enjoy its rich flavor and moist texture.

Tips for Making Classic Chocolate Cake:

- **Cocoa Powder:** Use high-quality unsweetened cocoa powder for the best chocolate flavor.

- **Boiling Water:** The boiling water helps to bloom the cocoa powder and create a smooth batter. Don't skip this step.

- **Room Temperature Ingredients:** Bringing eggs and milk to room temperature helps them incorporate better into the batter, resulting in a more uniform cake texture.

- **Storage:** Store leftover cake in an airtight container at room temperature for up to 3 days, or refrigerate for longer freshness.

This classic chocolate cake recipe is perfect for birthdays, celebrations, or any occasion where you want to indulge in a decadent chocolate treat. Enjoy baking and savoring this irresistible dessert!

34) Biscotti

Biscotti, an Italian twice-baked cookie, is known for its crisp texture and delicious flavors. Traditionally enjoyed with coffee or tea, biscotti are perfect for dunking. Here's a recipe to make classic biscotti at home:

Ingredients:

- 2 cups (250g) all-purpose flour
- 1 cup (200g) granulated sugar
- 1 teaspoon baking powder
- 1/4 teaspoon salt
- 3 large eggs
- 1 teaspoon vanilla extract
- 1 cup (150g) almonds, chopped (or other nuts/dried fruits of your choice)

- 1/2 cup (85g) semisweet or dark chocolate chips (optional, for dipping)

Instructions:

1. **Preheat the Oven:**
   - Preheat your oven to 350°F (175°C). Line a baking sheet with parchment paper or a silicone baking mat.

2. **Mix Dry Ingredients:**
   - In a large mixing bowl, whisk together flour, sugar, baking powder, and salt.

3. **Prepare Dough:**
   - In a separate bowl, beat eggs and vanilla extract together until well combined.
   - Gradually add the egg mixture to the dry ingredients, stirring until a stiff dough forms.
   - Fold in chopped almonds (or other nuts/dried fruits).

4. **Shape the Dough:**
   - Divide the dough in half. On a lightly floured surface, shape each half into a log about 12 inches long and 2 inches wide.

Place the logs on the prepared baking sheet, spaced apart.

5. **First Bake:**
    - Bake in the preheated oven for 25-30 minutes, or until the logs are firm to the touch and lightly browned.

6. **Cool and Slice:**
    - Remove the logs from the oven and let them cool on the baking sheet for 10-15 minutes.
    - Reduce the oven temperature to 325°F (160°C).
    - Using a serrated knife, carefully slice each log diagonally into 1/2-inch thick slices.

7. **Second Bake:**
    - Arrange the biscotti slices cut-side down on the baking sheet. Return to the oven and bake for 10-12 minutes, or until the biscotti are golden and crisp.

8. **Optional Chocolate Dip:**
    - If desired, melt chocolate chips in the microwave or over a double boiler until smooth.

- Dip one end of each cooled biscotti into the melted chocolate. Place on parchment paper to set.

9. **Cool and Store:**
    - Allow the biscotti to cool completely on a wire rack before serving or storing.

Tips for Making Biscotti:

- **Variations:** Experiment with different add-ins such as dried cranberries, pistachios, or orange zest to customize the flavors.

- **Texture:** For a crunchier biscotti, bake them longer during the second bake. If you prefer a softer texture, reduce the baking time.

- **Storage:** Store biscotti in an airtight container at room temperature for up to two weeks. They also freeze well for longer storage.

- **Serve:** Enjoy biscotti with coffee, tea. They make a delightful homemade gift or treat for gatherings.

Homemade biscotti are a delightful treat that pairs perfectly with your favorite hot beverage. Enjoy the crisp texture and customizable flavors of these classic Italian cookies!

35) *Traditional Baklava*

Baklava is a rich and sweet pastry made of layers of filo dough filled with chopped nuts and sweetened with honey or syrup. This Mediterranean and Middle Eastern dessert is known for its delicate layers and indulgent flavors. Here's how you can make traditional baklava at home:

Ingredients:

For the Baklava:

- 1 package (16 ounces) filo dough, thawed if frozen
- 1 and 1/2 cups (340g) unsalted butter, melted
- 3 cups (340g) mixed nuts (such as walnuts, pistachios, and almonds), finely chopped
- 1 teaspoon ground cinnamon
- 1/4 teaspoon ground cloves
- 1 cup (200g) granulated sugar
- 1 cup (240ml) water
- 1/2 cup (120ml) honey
- 1 tablespoon lemon juice
- 1 cinnamon stick (optional, for syrup)

Instructions:

1. **Prepare the Nuts:**

   - In a bowl, combine the chopped nuts with ground cinnamon and ground cloves. Set aside.

2. **Prepare the Syrup:**

   - In a saucepan, combine sugar, water, honey, lemon juice, and cinnamon stick (if using). Bring to a boil over medium-high heat, stirring occasionally. Reduce heat and simmer for 10 minutes until slightly thickened. Remove from heat and let cool. Once cooled, discard the cinnamon stick.

3. **Prepare the Filo Dough:**

   - Preheat your oven to 350°F (175°C). Grease a 9x13-inch baking dish with melted butter.

   - Carefully unroll the filo dough and cover it with a damp towel to prevent drying out while you work. Place one sheet of filo dough in the prepared baking dish and brush with melted butter. Repeat until you have 8-10 layers of filo dough.

4. **Add the Nut Mixture:**

- Sprinkle a generous amount of the nut mixture evenly over the buttered filo layers.
- Continue layering the filo dough sheets, brushing each layer with melted butter and sprinkling with nuts, until all the nuts are used up. Finish with a final layer of filo dough, brushing generously with butter.

5. **Cut and Bake:**
    - Using a sharp knife, carefully cut the baklava into diamond or square shapes. This will help the syrup penetrate evenly after baking.
    - Bake in the preheated oven for 45-50 minutes, or until golden brown and crisp.

6. **Syrup the Baklava:**
    - Remove the baklava from the oven and immediately pour the cooled syrup over the hot baklava, ensuring it covers all the cuts and edges.

7. **Cool and Serve:**
    - Allow the baklava to cool completely in the baking dish. This allows the flavors to

meld and the syrup to soak into the layers.

- Once cooled, carefully transfer the baklava pieces to a serving platter. Serve at room temperature and enjoy the rich, sweet flavors of traditional baklava.

Tips for Making Traditional Baklava:

- **Filo Dough Handling:** Work quickly with filo dough and keep it covered with a damp cloth to prevent drying out.

- **Nut Variations:** Customize the nut filling with your favorite nuts or a combination of nuts such as almonds, walnuts, pistachios, or even pecans.

- **Syrup Soaking:** The baklava should be hot from the oven when you pour the cooled syrup over it. This ensures that the pastry absorbs the syrup and stays moist.

- **Storage:** Store baklava in an airtight container at room temperature. It can stay fresh for several days and its flavors often improve with time.

Traditional baklava is a delightful dessert that combines crispy layers of filo with a sweet and nutty filling, soaked in a honey-infused syrup. Enjoy this classic treat as part of your next gathering or special occasion!

36) Lemon Tart

A lemon tart is a delightful dessert known for its tangy lemon filling and buttery crust. Here's a recipe to create a delicious lemon tart from scratch:

Ingredients:

For the Tart Crust:

- 1 and 1/4 cups (155g) all-purpose flour
- 1/4 cup (50g) granulated sugar
- 1/4 teaspoon salt
- 1/2 cup (115g) unsalted butter, cold and cut into cubes
- 1 large egg yolk
- 1-2 tablespoons ice water

For the Lemon Filling:

- 3/4 cup (150g) granulated sugar
- 1/2 cup (120ml) fresh lemon juice (from about 3-4 lemons)
- 1 tablespoon lemon zest (from about 2 lemons)
- 4 large eggs

- 1/2 cup (120ml) heavy cream
- Pinch of salt

For garnish (optional):

- Powdered sugar, for dusting
- Whipped cream or fresh berries, for serving

Instructions:

1. **Make the Tart Crust:**
    - In a food processor, combine flour, sugar, and salt. Pulse to mix.
    - Add cold butter cubes and pulse until the mixture resembles coarse crumbs.
    - Add egg yolk and pulse until the dough starts to come together. If needed, add ice water, one tablespoon at a time, until the dough forms into a ball.
    - Flatten the dough into a disk, wrap tightly in plastic wrap, and refrigerate for at least 1 hour, or up to 2 days.

2. **Preheat and Prepare:**
    - Preheat your oven to 375°F (190°C). Lightly grease a 9-inch tart pan with removable bottom.

3. **Roll Out and Shape the Crust:**
    - On a lightly floured surface, roll out the chilled dough into a circle about 12 inches in diameter and 1/8 inch thick.
    - Carefully transfer the rolled dough to the prepared tart pan. Press the dough into the bottom and sides of the pan. Trim any excess dough.
    - Prick the bottom of the crust with a fork to prevent bubbling during baking.

4. **Blind Bake the Crust:**
    - Line the tart crust with parchment paper or aluminum foil and fill with pie weights, dried beans, or rice.
    - Bake in the preheated oven for 15-18 minutes, or until the edges are lightly golden.
    - Remove the parchment paper and weights, and bake for an additional 5-7 minutes, or until the bottom of the crust is dry and golden brown.

5. **Prepare the Lemon Filling:**
    - In a medium bowl, whisk together sugar, lemon juice, lemon zest, eggs, heavy

cream, and a pinch of salt until smooth and well combined.

6. **Bake the Tart:**

    o Reduce the oven temperature to 325°F (160°C).

    o Pour the lemon filling into the pre-baked tart crust.

    o Bake for 25-30 minutes, or until the filling is set but still slightly jiggly in the center.

7. **Cool and Garnish:**

    o Allow the lemon tart to cool completely on a wire rack. Once cooled, refrigerate for at least 2 hours to chill and set the filling.

    o Before serving, dust the tart with powdered sugar and garnish with whipped cream or fresh berries if desired.

Tips for Making Lemon Tart:

- **Fresh Lemon Juice:** Use freshly squeezed lemon juice for the best flavor. Strain the juice to remove any pulp or seeds.

- **Chilling:** Chilling the tart after baking helps the filling set properly and enhances the flavors.

- **Storage:** Store leftover lemon tart covered in the refrigerator for up to 3 days. The crust may soften slightly over time, but it will still be delicious.

- **Serve:** Enjoy slices of lemon tart on its own or with a dollop of whipped cream or a side of fresh berries for a refreshing and tangy dessert.

This lemon tart recipe yields a wonderfully tart and creamy filling nestled in a crisp, buttery crust—a perfect balance of flavors for any occasion. Enjoy making and sharing this delightful dessert with family and friends!

37) Classic Apple Pie

Apple pie is a quintessential American dessert, loved for its sweet and spiced apple filling encased in a flaky pastry crust. Here's a traditional recipe that captures the essence of this beloved treat:

Ingredients:

For the Pie Crust:

- 2 and 1/2 cups (315g) all-purpose flour
- 1 teaspoon salt
- 1 tablespoon granulated sugar

- 1 cup (226g) unsalted butter, cold and cut into cubes
- 6-8 tablespoons ice water

For the Apple Filling:

- 6-7 large apples (such as Granny Smith or Honeycrisp), peeled, cored, and thinly sliced
- 1/2 cup (100g) granulated sugar
- 1/4 cup (50g) light brown sugar, packed
- 1 teaspoon ground cinnamon
- 1/4 teaspoon ground nutmeg (optional)
- 1/4 teaspoon salt
- 1 tablespoon lemon juice
- 2 tablespoons unsalted butter, cut into small pieces
- 1 tablespoon all-purpose flour (optional, to thicken filling)

For Assembly:

- 1 egg, beaten (for egg wash)
- Granulated sugar, for sprinkling

Instructions:

1. **Make the Pie Crust:**

    - In a large mixing bowl, whisk together flour, salt, and sugar.

    - Add cold cubed butter to the flour mixture. Use a pastry cutter or your fingertips to quickly work the butter into the flour until the mixture resembles coarse crumbs with some larger pea-sized pieces of butter.

    - Gradually add ice water, one tablespoon at a time, tossing with a fork to incorporate. Add just enough water for the dough to come together when squeezed. Do not overmix.

    - Divide the dough into two equal portions and flatten each into a disk. Wrap each disk tightly in plastic wrap and refrigerate for at least 1 hour, or up to 2 days.

2. **Prepare the Apple Filling:**

    - In a large bowl, combine sliced apples, granulated sugar, brown sugar, cinnamon, nutmeg (if using), salt, and lemon juice. Toss until the apples are evenly coated. If the filling is very juicy, sprinkle flour over the apples and toss to coat (optional).

3. **Roll Out the Pie Crust:**

- Preheat your oven to 400°F (200°C). Lightly grease a 9-inch pie dish with butter.

- On a lightly floured surface, roll out one disk of chilled dough into a circle about 12 inches in diameter. Transfer the rolled dough to the prepared pie dish, gently pressing it into the bottom and up the sides.

4. **Assemble the Pie:**

    - Fill the pie crust with the prepared apple filling, mounding slightly in the center. Dot the filling with small pieces of butter.

    - Roll out the second disk of dough into a circle about 12 inches in diameter. Place it over the filling. Trim any excess dough, leaving about a 1-inch overhang. Fold the overhang under the bottom crust, pressing to seal. Crimp the edges with a fork or your fingers.

5. **Bake the Pie:**

    - Brush the top crust with beaten egg wash and sprinkle with granulated sugar.

    - Cut a few small slits in the top crust to allow steam to escape during baking.

- Place the pie on a baking sheet to catch any drips and bake in the preheated oven for 45-55 minutes, or until the crust is golden brown and the filling is bubbly.

6. **Cool and Serve:**
    - Allow the apple pie to cool on a wire rack for at least 2 hours before slicing and serving. This helps the filling set and makes for easier slicing.

Tips for Making Classic Apple Pie:

- **Apple Selection:** Choose firm and tart apples like Granny Smith or Honeycrisp for the best texture and flavor in your pie.

- **Thickening Agent:** If your apple filling is very juicy, sprinkle flour over the apples before filling the pie crust. This helps absorb excess moisture during baking.

- **Storage:** Store leftover apple pie covered at room temperature for up to 2 days. For longer storage, refrigerate the pie, but bring it to room temperature or warm slightly before serving.

- **Serve with:** Enjoy a slice of apple pie on its own or with a scoop of vanilla ice cream or a dollop of whipped cream for an extra treat.

This classic apple pie recipe yields a perfect balance of sweet apples and warm spices wrapped in a buttery, flaky crust—a timeless dessert that's sure to delight everyone at your table.

38) Mini Fruit Tarts

Mini fruit tarts are delightful, bite-sized desserts that showcase a colorful array of fresh fruits atop a creamy custard, all nestled in a crisp pastry shell. Here's a recipe to create these elegant treats:

Ingredients:

For the Tart Shells:

- 1 and 1/4 cups (155g) all-purpose flour
- 1/2 cup (113g) unsalted butter, cold and cut into cubes
- 1/4 cup (50g) granulated sugar
- 1/4 teaspoon salt
- 1 large egg yolk
- 1-2 tablespoons ice water

For the Pastry Cream:

- 1 cup (240ml) whole milk
- 1/2 cup (100g) granulated sugar

- 3 large egg yolks
- 2 tablespoons cornstarch
- 1/4 teaspoon salt
- 1 teaspoon vanilla extract

For Assembly:

- Assorted fresh fruits (such as berries, kiwi, grapes, mango, etc.), washed and sliced
- Apricot jam or fruit glaze for brushing (optional)

Instructions:

1. **Make the Tart Shells:**
    - In a food processor, pulse together flour, sugar, and salt until combined.
    - Add cold cubed butter and pulse until the mixture resembles coarse crumbs.
    - Add egg yolk and pulse until the dough starts to come together. If needed, add ice water, one tablespoon at a time, until the dough forms into a ball.
    - Flatten the dough into a disk, wrap tightly in plastic wrap, and refrigerate for at least 1 hour, or up to 2 days.

2. **Prepare the Pastry Cream:**

    - In a medium saucepan, heat milk over medium heat until steaming (do not boil).

    - In a separate bowl, whisk together sugar, egg yolks, cornstarch, and salt until smooth.

    - Gradually whisk the hot milk into the egg mixture. Return the mixture to the saucepan.

    - Cook over medium heat, whisking constantly, until the mixture thickens and comes to a boil. Boil for 1 minute, then remove from heat.

    - Stir in vanilla extract. Transfer the pastry cream to a bowl and cover with plastic wrap, pressing the wrap directly onto the surface of the cream to prevent a skin from forming. Chill in the refrigerator until cold.

3. **Bake the Tart Shells:**

    - Preheat your oven to 375°F (190°C). Lightly grease a mini tart pan with removable bottoms.

    - On a lightly floured surface, roll out the chilled dough to about 1/8-inch thickness.

Cut out rounds slightly larger than the tart molds.

- Press the dough into each tart mold, trimming any excess. Prick the bottoms with a fork.
- Place a small piece of parchment paper or foil into each tart shell and fill with pie weights, dried beans, or rice.
- Bake for 10-12 minutes, or until the edges are lightly golden. Remove the weights and parchment paper/foil, and bake for an additional 5-7 minutes, or until the bottoms are dry and golden brown.
- Allow the tart shells to cool completely in the pan on a wire rack.

4. **Assemble the Mini Fruit Tarts:**
    - Spoon chilled pastry cream into each cooled tart shell, filling just below the rim.
    - Arrange assorted fresh fruit slices on top of the pastry cream in a decorative pattern.
    - Optional: Warm apricot jam or fruit glaze in a small saucepan until melted. Brush over the fruit to create a shiny finish.

5. **Chill and Serve:**

    - Refrigerate the mini fruit tarts for at least 1 hour to set the pastry cream and chill the fruit.

    - Serve chilled and enjoy these delightful mini fruit tarts as a refreshing and elegant dessert.

Tips for Making Mini Fruit Tarts:

- **Variety of Fruits:** Use a variety of colorful and seasonal fruits for an attractive presentation. Berries, kiwi, grapes, mango, and citrus fruits work well.

- **Pastry Cream Consistency:** Ensure the pastry cream is chilled and thickened before filling the tart shells to prevent it from being too runny.

- **Glazing:** Brushing the fruit with apricot jam or fruit glaze adds shine and prevents fruits like apples and bananas from browning.

- **Make Ahead:** You can prepare the tart shells and pastry cream ahead of time. Assemble the tarts shortly before serving for the freshest presentation.

These mini fruit tarts are perfect for parties, gatherings, or simply as a treat for yourself. Enjoy the combination of crisp pastry, creamy custard, and fresh fruits in every delightful bite!

39) Creamy Rice Pudding

Creamy rice pudding is a comforting and classic dessert enjoyed in various cultures around the world. Here's a recipe to make a delicious and comforting creamy rice pudding:

Ingredients:

- 1 cup (200g) medium or short-grain white rice
- 4 cups (960ml) whole milk
- 1/2 cup (100g) granulated sugar
- 1/4 teaspoon salt
- 1 teaspoon vanilla extract
- 1/2 teaspoon ground cinnamon (optional)
- 1/4 teaspoon ground nutmeg (optional)
- 1/2 cup (120ml) heavy cream
- Raisins, dried fruits, or nuts (optional, for garnish)

Instructions:

1. **Prepare the Rice:**

- Rinse the rice under cold water until the water runs clear. This removes excess starch and prevents the rice from becoming too sticky.

2. **Cook the Rice:**

    - In a large saucepan, combine the rinsed rice and milk over medium-high heat. Bring to a boil, then reduce the heat to low.

    - Stirring frequently, simmer the rice and milk mixture uncovered for about 25-30 minutes, or until the rice is tender and the mixture has thickened to a creamy consistency.

3. **Add Sugar and Flavorings:**

    - Stir in the granulated sugar, salt, vanilla extract, ground cinnamon (if using), and ground nutmeg (if using). Continue to cook for another 5-10 minutes, stirring occasionally, until the sugar is dissolved and the pudding thickens further.

4. **Finish with Heavy Cream:**

    - Remove the saucepan from heat and stir in the heavy cream. This adds richness and a smooth texture to the rice pudding.

5. **Serve and Garnish:**
    - Spoon the creamy rice pudding into serving bowls or glasses. If desired, garnish with a sprinkle of ground cinnamon, raisins, dried fruits, or nuts for added flavor and texture.

6. **Chill (Optional):**
    - Serve the rice pudding warm or chilled. To chill, cover with plastic wrap directly touching the surface of the pudding to prevent a skin from forming. Refrigerate for at least 1 hour before serving.

Tips for Making Creamy Rice Pudding:

- **Rice Selection:** Use medium or short-grain white rice for the best texture. These rice varieties release starch as they cook, contributing to the creamy consistency of the pudding.

- **Stirring:** Stir the rice pudding frequently, especially towards the end of cooking, to prevent the rice from sticking to the bottom of the pan and to ensure even cooking.

- **Flavor Variations:** Customize your rice pudding by adding different flavorings such as lemon zest, almond extract, or a splash of rum or brandy for a grown-up version.

- **Texture Adjustment:** If the rice pudding becomes too thick upon cooling, simply stir in a little more milk or cream until it reaches your desired consistency.

- **Storage:** Leftover rice pudding can be stored covered in the refrigerator for up to 3 days. Reheat gently on the stovetop or in the microwave before serving.

This creamy rice pudding recipe offers a comforting and indulgent dessert that's perfect for any occasion. Enjoy the warm, comforting flavors and smooth texture of homemade rice pudding with this easy-to-follow recipe!

40) Crème Brûlée

Crème brûlée, with its rich custard base and caramelized sugar topping, is a decadent French dessert that delights with its contrasting textures of creamy and crunchy. Here's how to make this classic dessert:

Ingredients:

- 6 large egg yolks
- 1/2 cup (100g) granulated sugar
- 2 cups (480ml) heavy cream
- 1 teaspoon vanilla extract
- Pinch of salt

- 3-4 tablespoons granulated sugar (for caramelizing)

Instructions:

1. **Preheat Oven and Prepare Ramekins:**
   - Preheat your oven to 325°F (160°C). Place 6 ramekins (about 6-ounce capacity each) in a baking dish or roasting pan.

2. **Prepare the Custard:**
   - In a mixing bowl, whisk together egg yolks and sugar until well combined and slightly thickened.
   - In a saucepan, heat heavy cream over medium heat until it just begins to simmer. Remove from heat.
   - Gradually pour the hot cream into the egg yolk mixture, whisking constantly, until smooth and well combined. Stir in vanilla extract and a pinch of salt.

3. **Bake the Custard:**
   - Pour the custard mixture evenly into the ramekins. Fill the baking dish or roasting pan with enough hot water to come halfway up the sides of the ramekins, creating a water bath (bain-marie).

- Carefully transfer the baking dish to the preheated oven. Bake for 30-35 minutes, or until the custards are set around the edges but still slightly jiggly in the center.

4. **Chill the Custards:**
    - Remove the ramekins from the water bath and let them cool to room temperature. Cover with plastic wrap and refrigerate for at least 2 hours, or overnight, until thoroughly chilled and set.

5. **Caramelize the Sugar Topping:**
    - Just before serving, sprinkle about 1/2 tablespoon of granulated sugar evenly over the surface of each custard.
    - Using a kitchen torch, carefully caramelize the sugar until it melts and forms a golden-brown crust. Alternatively, place the ramekins under a preheated broiler for 1-2 minutes, watching closely, until the sugar caramelizes.

6. **Serve Immediately:**
    - Let the crème brûlée sit for a few minutes to allow the caramelized sugar to harden. Serve immediately and enjoy the contrast

between the creamy custard and the crisp caramel topping.

Tips for Making Crème Brûlée:

- **Egg Yolks:** Use only egg yolks for a rich and creamy custard base. Save the egg whites for another recipe, such as meringues or macarons.

- **Water Bath:** Baking the custards in a water bath helps ensure gentle and even cooking, preventing them from curdling or overcooking.

- **Caramelizing Sugar:** For best results, use a kitchen torch for caramelizing the sugar. Move the flame in a circular motion to evenly melt and brown the sugar without burning it.

- **Make-Ahead:** You can prepare the custards a day ahead and keep them refrigerated, covered with plastic wrap, until ready to caramelize and serve.

- **Flavor Variations:** Add a twist to your crème brûlée by infusing the cream with flavors like citrus zest, cinnamon, or a splash of liqueur such as Grand Marnier or Amaretto.

This crème brûlée recipe yields a luscious dessert with its creamy custard base and crisp caramelized sugar topping—a timeless treat that impresses with its elegant presentation and rich flavor.

41) Chocolate Mousse

Chocolate mousse is a luxurious and airy dessert that combines the richness of chocolate with the lightness of whipped cream. Here's a recipe to create a decadent chocolate mousse:

Ingredients:

- 8 ounces (about 225g) semi-sweet or bittersweet chocolate, chopped
- 1/2 cup (120ml) heavy cream
- 4 large eggs, separated
- 1/4 cup (50g) granulated sugar
- 1 teaspoon vanilla extract
- Pinch of salt
- Whipped cream, chocolate shavings, or berries for garnish (optional)

Instructions:

1. **Melt the Chocolate:**
    - In a heatproof bowl set over a saucepan of simmering water (double boiler method), melt the chopped chocolate with the heavy cream. Stir occasionally until

smooth and completely melted. Remove from heat and let cool slightly.

2. **Prepare the Egg Yolks:**

    - In a separate bowl, whisk together the egg yolks, granulated sugar, vanilla extract, and a pinch of salt until pale and slightly thickened.

    - Gradually whisk the melted chocolate mixture into the egg yolk mixture until smooth and well combined.

3. **Whip the Egg Whites:**

    - In another bowl, using a clean and dry whisk or electric mixer with a whisk attachment, beat the egg whites until stiff peaks form.

4. **Combine and Chill:**

    - Gently fold the whipped egg whites into the chocolate mixture in two additions, using a spatula. Be careful not to deflate the egg whites.

    - Divide the chocolate mousse evenly among serving dishes or glasses. Cover with plastic wrap and refrigerate for at least 2 hours, or until set and chilled.

5. **Serve:**

    o Before serving, garnish each chocolate mousse with a dollop of whipped cream, chocolate shavings, or berries if desired.

Tips for Making Chocolate Mousse:

- **Chocolate Selection:** Use high-quality chocolate for the best flavor. Semi-sweet or bittersweet chocolate with at least 60% cocoa content works well.

- **Egg Separation:** Ensure no egg yolks get into the egg whites when separating them, as any fat can prevent the whites from whipping properly.

- **Folding Technique:** When folding the whipped egg whites into the chocolate mixture, use a gentle motion to maintain the mousse's light and airy texture.

- **Chilling Time:** Refrigerate the chocolate mousse for at least 2 hours to allow it to set properly. This also enhances the flavor and texture.

- **Storage:** Store leftover chocolate mousse covered in the refrigerator for up to 2 days. Serve chilled.

Enjoy the indulgent and velvety-smooth texture of homemade chocolate mousse with this easy-to-follow recipe. It's perfect for special occasions or whenever you crave a luxurious chocolate dessert!

PART 7: SPECIAL OCCASIONS

Celebrate special moments with recipes designed to elevate any gathering. Whether you're preparing for holiday feasts, family gatherings, or elegant dinner parties, this section provides inspiring dishes that bring people together and create lasting memories.

Large Batch Cooking

Large batch cooking is a practical approach for preparing meals in advance, whether for feeding a crowd, stocking up on freezer meals, or simplifying weekday dinners. Here's a guide to mastering large batch cooking effectively:

Benefits of Large Batch Cooking:

1. **Efficiency and Time-Saving:** Large batch cooking allows you to prepare multiple meals at once, saving time on meal prep throughout the week. It's particularly useful for busy schedules or when cooking for a large family.

2. **Cost-Effective:** Buying ingredients in bulk often costs less per serving. By cooking in large batches, you can also take advantage of sales and discounts, reducing overall grocery expenses.

3. **Minimizes Waste:** Planning and cooking in bulk can help minimize food waste. You can portion out meals for future use, reducing the likelihood of unused ingredients going bad.

4. **Consistent Quality:** Cooking in larger quantities can sometimes improve the flavor of certain dishes as flavors meld together over time, especially in stews, soups, and casseroles.

Tips for Successful Large Batch Cooking:

1. **Plan Ahead:**
   - Choose recipes that freeze well or can be stored for several days without compromising quality. Consider dishes like soups, stews, casseroles, pasta sauces, and curries.

2. **Use Proper Equipment:**
   - Invest in large pots, pans, and storage containers that can accommodate the volume of food you plan to cook. A slow cooker or pressure cooker can also be helpful for certain recipes.

3. **Organize and Prep Ingredients:**
   - Prep ingredients in advance, such as chopping vegetables or marinating meats. This streamlines the cooking process and ensures everything is ready when you start cooking.

4. **Scale Recipes Appropriately:**
   - Adjust recipes to fit the number of servings you need. Double or triple ingredient quantities accordingly, but pay attention to cooking times and adjust if necessary.

5. **Label and Store Properly:**

- After cooking, portion out meals into individual containers or freezer-safe bags. Label each with the contents and date of preparation for easy identification later.

6. **Safety and Hygiene:**

    - Practice safe food handling practices, especially when working with larger quantities of food. Ensure meats are cooked to safe temperatures and leftovers are cooled and stored promptly.

Example Recipe for Large Batch Cooking:

42) Beef and Vegetable Stew

Ingredients:

- 3 pounds (1.4 kg) stewing beef, cut into cubes
- 2 tablespoons olive oil
- 4 large carrots, peeled and sliced
- 4 celery stalks, sliced
- 2 onions, chopped
- 4 cloves garlic, minced
- 1 cup (240ml) Vinegar (optional)
- 6 cups (1.5 liters) beef broth

- 2 bay leaves
- 1 teaspoon dried thyme
- Salt and pepper, to taste
- 4 large potatoes, peeled and diced
- 2 cups (300g) frozen peas

Instructions:

1. In a large pot or Dutch oven, heat olive oil over medium-high heat. Brown the beef cubes in batches until browned on all sides. Remove and set aside.

2. In the same pot, add carrots, celery, onions, and garlic. Cook, stirring occasionally, until vegetables are softened, about 5-7 minutes.

3. Pour in vinegar (if using), scraping up any browned bits from the bottom of the pot. Cook for 2-3 minutes until slightly reduced.

4. Return the beef to the pot. Add beef broth, bay leaves, thyme, salt, and pepper. Bring to a boil, then reduce heat to low, cover, and simmer for 1.5 to 2 hours, stirring occasionally, until beef is tender.

5. Add diced potatoes and continue to simmer, uncovered, for an additional 30-40 minutes, or

until potatoes are cooked through and stew has thickened slightly.

6. Stir in frozen peas and cook for another 5 minutes until peas are heated through. Adjust seasoning if necessary.

7. Allow the stew to cool slightly before portioning into containers for storage or serving.

This hearty beef and vegetable stew is perfect for large batch cooking. It can be portioned into individual servings and stored in the refrigerator for up to 3 days or frozen for longer storage. Reheat portions as needed for quick and satisfying meals throughout the week.

Large batch cooking not only saves time and money but also allows you to enjoy homemade meals with minimal effort on busy days. Experiment with different recipes and find what works best for your household's needs and preferences!

Potluck Favorites

Potlucks are gatherings where guests bring dishes to share, creating a diverse spread of foods. Here are some crowd-pleasing potluck favorites that are easy to make and transport:

43) Macaroni and Cheese

Ingredients:

- 1 pound (450g) elbow macaroni
- 1/2 cup (115g) unsalted butter
- 1/2 cup (60g) all-purpose flour
- 4 cups (960ml) whole milk
- 2 cups (200g) shredded sharp cheddar cheese
- 1 cup (100g) shredded mozzarella cheese
- 1 cup (100g) shredded Gruyère cheese
- Salt and pepper, to taste
- 1/2 cup (50g) grated Parmesan cheese
- 1 cup (100g) breadcrumbs
- Chopped parsley, for garnish (optional)

Instructions:

1. Cook the elbow macaroni according to package instructions until al dente. Drain and set aside.

2. In a large saucepan, melt the butter over medium heat. Stir in the flour and cook for 1-2 minutes until smooth and bubbly, stirring constantly.

3. Gradually whisk in the milk and cook, stirring constantly, until the sauce thickens and begins to simmer, about 5-7 minutes.

4. Remove the saucepan from the heat and stir in the shredded cheddar, mozzarella, and Gruyère cheeses until melted and smooth. Season with salt and pepper to taste.

5. Add the cooked macaroni to the cheese sauce and stir until well combined.

6. In a small bowl, combine the grated Parmesan cheese and breadcrumbs.

7. Transfer the macaroni and cheese mixture to a large baking dish. Sprinkle the breadcrumb mixture evenly over the top.

8. Bake in a preheated oven at 350°F (175°C) for 25-30 minutes, or until the top is golden brown and the cheese is bubbly.

9. Garnish with chopped parsley if desired, and serve hot.

44) Buffalo Chicken Dip

Ingredients:

- 2 cups (300g) shredded cooked chicken
- 8 ounces (225g) cream cheese, softened
- 1/2 cup (120ml) hot sauce (such as Frank's RedHot)

- 1/2 cup (120ml) ranch or blue cheese dressing
- 1 cup (100g) shredded cheddar cheese
- 1/2 cup (60g) crumbled blue cheese (optional)
- Tortilla chips, celery sticks, or crackers, for serving

Instructions:

1. Preheat your oven to 350°F (175°C).
2. In a mixing bowl, combine shredded chicken, cream cheese, hot sauce, ranch or blue cheese dressing, and shredded cheddar cheese. Mix until well combined.
3. Transfer the mixture to a baking dish and spread it evenly.
4. Sprinkle crumbled blue cheese (if using) over the top.
5. Bake in the preheated oven for 20-25 minutes, or until the dip is heated through and bubbly around the edges.
6. Remove from the oven and let cool slightly before serving.
7. Serve with tortilla chips, celery sticks, or crackers for dipping.

45) Caprese Salad Skewers

Ingredients:

- Cherry tomatoes
- Fresh mozzarella balls (bocconcini)
- Fresh basil leaves
- Balsamic glaze
- Salt and pepper, to taste
- Wooden skewers

Instructions:

1. Thread cherry tomatoes, mozzarella balls, and fresh basil leaves onto wooden skewers, alternating the ingredients.
2. Arrange the skewers on a serving platter.
3. Drizzle with balsamic glaze and season with salt and pepper to taste.
4. Serve chilled or at room temperature.

Tips for Potluck Cooking:

- **Transportation:** Choose dishes that are easy to transport and serve. Use covered containers for hot dishes and trays with lids for cold dishes.

- **Allergies and Preferences:** Consider dietary restrictions and preferences of guests when selecting recipes. Provide options for vegetarian, gluten-free, or dairy-free diets if possible.

- **Preparation:** Prepare dishes ahead of time, if possible, and reheat or assemble just before serving to ensure freshness.

- **Labeling:** Label dishes with ingredients, especially if they contain common allergens like nuts or dairy.

Potluck favorites like macaroni and cheese, buffalo chicken dip, and caprese salad skewers are sure to be a hit at any gathering. Enjoy the camaraderie of sharing homemade dishes with friends and family!

Kid-Friendly Recipes

When cooking for kids, it's essential to create dishes that are not only nutritious but also appealing and easy for little ones to enjoy. Here are some kid-friendly recipes that are sure to please even the pickiest eaters:

46) Mini Pizza Bites

Ingredients:

- English muffins or small pizza dough rounds
- Pizza sauce

- Shredded mozzarella cheese

- Mini pepperoni slices or other favorite toppings (diced bell peppers, sliced olives, etc.)

Instructions:

1. Preheat your oven to 375°F (190°C).

2. Split the English muffins in half (if using) and arrange them on a baking sheet.

3. Spread a tablespoon of pizza sauce on each muffin half.

4. Sprinkle shredded mozzarella cheese over the sauce.

5. Add mini pepperoni slices or other toppings as desired.

6. Bake in the preheated oven for 10-12 minutes, or until the cheese is melted and bubbly.

7. Let cool slightly before serving.

47) *Chicken and Vegetable Skewers*

Ingredients:

- Chicken breast or thigh meat, cut into bite-sized pieces

- Bell peppers (red, yellow, green), cut into chunks
- Cherry tomatoes
- Zucchini or squash, cut into rounds
- Olive oil
- Salt and pepper, to taste
- Wooden skewers

Instructions:

1. Preheat a grill or grill pan over medium-high heat.
2. Thread chicken pieces and vegetables alternately onto wooden skewers.
3. Brush skewers with olive oil and season with salt and pepper.
4. Grill skewers for 8-10 minutes, turning occasionally, until chicken is cooked through and vegetables are tender.
5. Serve hot with a side of rice or salad.

48) Veggie Quesadillas

Ingredients:

- Flour tortillas

- Shredded cheddar cheese
- Mixed vegetables (bell peppers, corn, black beans, spinach)
- Olive oil or cooking spray

Instructions:

1. Heat a non-stick skillet or griddle over medium heat.
2. Place one tortilla in the skillet and sprinkle with shredded cheese.
3. Add a layer of mixed vegetables over the cheese.
4. Top with another tortilla and press down gently.
5. Cook for 2-3 minutes per side, or until tortillas are golden brown and cheese is melted.
6. Remove from skillet and let cool slightly before cutting into wedges.
7. Serve with salsa, guacamole, or sour cream for dipping.

49) Banana Oatmeal Cookies

Ingredients:

- 2 ripe bananas, mashed

- 1 cup rolled oats
- 1/4 cup peanut butter or almond butter
- 1/4 cup chocolate chips or raisins (optional)
- 1 teaspoon vanilla extract
- Pinch of cinnamon (optional)

Instructions:

1. Preheat your oven to 350°F (175°C). Line a baking sheet with parchment paper.
2. In a mixing bowl, combine mashed bananas, rolled oats, peanut butter, chocolate chips or raisins, vanilla extract, and cinnamon (if using). Mix until well combined.
3. Drop spoonfuls of the cookie dough onto the prepared baking sheet.
4. Flatten each cookie slightly with the back of a spoon.
5. Bake for 12-15 minutes, or until cookies are golden brown and set.
6. Let cool on the baking sheet for 5 minutes before transferring to a wire rack to cool completely.

These kid-friendly recipes are not only easy to make but also nutritious and delicious. Whether its mini pizza bites, chicken and vegetable skewers, veggie quesadillas, or banana oatmeal cookies, these dishes are sure to be a hit with children of all ages!

Elegant Dinner Parties

Hosting an elegant dinner party calls for dishes that are sophisticated, flavorful, and beautifully presented. Here are some impressive recipes to elevate your dinner party menu:

50) Herb-Crusted Rack of Lamb

Ingredients:

- 2 racks of lamb, trimmed (about 1 1/2 pounds each)
- Salt and freshly ground black pepper
- 2 tablespoons Dijon mustard
- 2 cloves garlic, minced
- 1 tablespoon fresh rosemary, finely chopped
- 1 tablespoon fresh thyme leaves, finely chopped
- 1 cup breadcrumbs (preferably Panko)
- 2 tablespoons olive oil

Instructions:

1. Preheat your oven to 400°F (200°C).

2. Season the racks of lamb generously with salt and pepper.

3. In a small bowl, mix together Dijon mustard, minced garlic, rosemary, and thyme.

4. Press the breadcrumb mixture onto the meaty side of each rack of lamb to coat evenly.

5. Heat olive oil in a large oven-safe skillet over medium-high heat. Sear the racks of lamb, meaty side down, for 3-4 minutes or until golden brown.

6. Transfer the skillet to the preheated oven and roast for 15-20 minutes, depending on desired doneness (medium-rare is recommended, with an internal temperature of 145°F or 63°C).

7. Remove from the oven and let the lamb rest for 5-10 minutes before slicing into chops and serving.

51) *Lobster Risotto*

Ingredients:

- 1 cup Arborio rice
- 4 cups seafood or chicken broth

- 2 tablespoons olive oil
- 1 shallot, finely chopped
- 1 garlic clove, minced
- 1/2 cup Vinegar
- 1/2 cup grated Parmesan cheese
- 2 lobster tails, cooked and chopped
- Salt and freshly ground black pepper
- Fresh parsley, chopped, for garnish

Instructions:

1. In a saucepan, bring the seafood or chicken broth to a simmer. Keep warm over low heat.
2. In a separate large saucepan or Dutch oven, heat olive oil over medium heat. Add shallot and garlic, sautéing until translucent, about 2-3 minutes.
3. Add Arborio rice to the pan, stirring to coat with the oil, for about 1 minute.
4. Pour in the vinegar, stirring constantly until absorbed.
5. Begin adding the warm broth, one ladleful at a time, stirring frequently and allowing each

addition to be absorbed before adding the next. Continue until the rice is creamy and tender, about 18-20 minutes.

6. Stir in grated Parmesan cheese and chopped lobster tails. Season with salt and pepper to taste.

7. Remove from heat and let stand for a few minutes. Serve risotto warm, garnished with chopped parsley.

52) Chocolate Soufflé

Ingredients:

- 4 ounces (115g) bittersweet chocolate, chopped
- 3 tablespoons unsalted butter, plus extra for greasing ramekins
- 1/4 cup granulated sugar, plus extra for coating ramekins
- 3 large egg yolks
- 4 large egg whites
- Pinch of salt
- Powdered sugar, for dusting

Instructions:

1. Preheat your oven to 375°F (190°C). Grease four 6-ounce ramekins with butter and dust with granulated sugar, tapping out any excess.

2. In a heatproof bowl set over a saucepan of simmering water (double boiler method), melt the chopped chocolate and butter, stirring until smooth. Remove from heat and let cool slightly.

3. Whisk egg yolks and 2 tablespoons of granulated sugar in a separate bowl until pale and thickened.

4. Gradually whisk the melted chocolate mixture into the egg yolk mixture until well combined.

5. In a clean, dry bowl, beat egg whites with a pinch of salt using an electric mixer until foamy. Gradually add remaining 2 tablespoons of granulated sugar, beating until stiff peaks form.

6. Gently fold the beaten egg whites into the chocolate mixture in two additions, using a spatula, until no streaks remain.

7. Divide the soufflé mixture evenly among the prepared ramekins. Run your thumb around the inside rim of each ramekin to create a shallow groove (this helps the soufflé rise evenly).

8. Place ramekins on a baking sheet and bake in the preheated oven for 12-15 minutes, or until

soufflés have risen and set, with a slightly soft center.

9. Dust with powdered sugar and serve immediately.

These elegant dinner party recipes, including herb-crusted rack of lamb, lobster risotto, and chocolate soufflé, are sure to impress your guests with their flavors and presentation.

Outdoor Barbecue

An outdoor barbecue is a perfect way to enjoy delicious grilled foods and the company of friends and family in a casual, relaxed setting. Here are some classic recipes and tips to make your barbecue a hit:

> *53) Grilled BBQ Chicken Drumsticks*

Ingredients:

- 8 chicken drumsticks
- Salt and freshly ground black pepper
- 1 cup BBQ sauce (store-bought or homemade)
- Vegetable oil, for grilling

Instructions:

1. Preheat your grill to medium-high heat.

2. Season chicken drumsticks generously with salt and pepper.

3. Oil the grill grates lightly to prevent sticking.

4. Place chicken drumsticks on the grill and cook for about 10 minutes, turning occasionally, until lightly charred on all sides.

5. Brush BBQ sauce over the drumsticks, coating evenly.

6. Continue grilling for another 5-10 minutes, basting occasionally with more BBQ sauce, until chicken is cooked through and juices run clear.

7. Remove from the grill and let rest for a few minutes before serving.

54) Grilled Corn on the Cob with Herb Butter

Ingredients:

- 4 ears of corn, husked

- 4 tablespoons unsalted butter, softened

- 1 tablespoon chopped fresh herbs (such as parsley, chives, or cilantro)

- Salt and freshly ground black pepper

Instructions:

1. Preheat grill to medium heat.
2. In a small bowl, mix together softened butter, chopped herbs, salt, and pepper.
3. Place corn on the grill and cook, turning occasionally, until kernels are tender and lightly charred, about 10-12 minutes.
4. Remove corn from the grill and immediately spread each ear with herb butter while still hot.
5. Serve warm.

55) *Grilled Veggie Skewers*

Ingredients:

- Assorted vegetables (bell peppers, zucchini, cherry tomatoes, mushrooms, red onion, etc.)
- Olive oil
- Salt and freshly ground black pepper
- Wooden or metal skewers

Instructions:

1. Preheat grill to medium-high heat.

2. Cut vegetables into bite-sized pieces, ensuring they are uniform for even cooking.

3. Thread vegetables onto skewers, alternating colors and varieties.

4. Brush skewers with olive oil and season with salt and pepper.

5. Grill skewers for 8-10 minutes, turning occasionally, until vegetables are tender and lightly charred.

6. Serve hot as a delicious side dish.

56) Grilled Pineapple with Honey and Cinnamon

Ingredients:

- 1 pineapple, peeled, cored, and cut into rings or wedges
- Honey
- Ground cinnamon

Instructions:

1. Preheat grill to medium-high heat.

2. Grill pineapple slices for 2-3 minutes per side, or until lightly caramelized grill marks appear.

3. Remove pineapple from the grill and drizzle with honey.

4. Sprinkle with ground cinnamon to taste.

5. Serve warm as a refreshing dessert or side dish.

Tips for a Successful Outdoor Barbecue:

- **Preparation:** Marinate meats ahead of time for enhanced flavor and tenderness.

- **Grilling:** Keep an eye on the grill temperature and adjust as needed to prevent burning.

- **Variety:** Offer a variety of meats, vegetables, and sides to accommodate different tastes and dietary preferences.

- **Safety:** Ensure food safety by using separate plates and utensils for raw and cooked foods.

With these delicious recipes and tips, your outdoor barbecue is sure to be a memorable gathering filled with great food and enjoyable moments shared with loved ones. Enjoy the flavors of grilled favorites and the relaxed atmosphere of outdoor dining!

Creating a delightful afternoon tea spread involves offering a selection of savory and sweet treats, along with a variety of teas to suit different tastes. Here's how you can assemble a classic afternoon tea spread:

57) Cucumber and Cream Cheese Sandwiches:

- Thinly sliced cucumber
- Cream cheese
- Salt and pepper
- White or whole wheat bread, crusts removed

Instructions:

1. Spread cream cheese evenly on slices of bread.
2. Arrange thinly sliced cucumber on half of the bread slices.
3. Season with salt and pepper.
4. Top with remaining bread slices and cut into triangles or rectangles.

58) Smoked Salmon and Dill Sandwiches:

- Smoked salmon slices
- Cream cheese or whipped butter
- Fresh dill
- Rye or pumpernickel bread, crusts removed

Instructions:

1. Spread cream cheese or whipped butter on slices of rye or pumpernickel bread.

2. Layer smoked salmon slices on half of the bread slices.

3. Garnish with fresh dill.

4. Top with remaining bread slices and cut into triangles.

59) Classic Scones with Clotted Cream and Jam

Ingredients:

- 2 cups all-purpose flour
- 1/4 cup granulated sugar
- 1 tablespoon baking powder
- 1/2 teaspoon salt
- 1/3 cup cold unsalted butter, cut into small pieces
- 1/2 cup raisins or currants (optional)
- 1/2 cup milk
- 1/4 cup heavy cream

- Clotted cream and strawberry jam, for serving

Instructions:

1. Preheat your oven to 400°F (200°C). Line a baking sheet with parchment paper.

2. In a large bowl, whisk together flour, sugar, baking powder, and salt.

3. Cut in the cold butter using a pastry blender or your fingertips until the mixture resembles coarse crumbs.

4. Stir in raisins or currants if using.

5. Make a well in the center and pour in the milk and heavy cream. Stir until the dough comes together.

6. Turn out the dough onto a lightly floured surface and knead gently a few times until smooth.

7. Pat the dough into a circle about 3/4 inch thick. Using a floured round cutter, cut out scones and place them on the prepared baking sheet.

8. Brush the tops of the scones with a little milk or cream for a golden finish.

9. Bake for 12-15 minutes, or until the scones are golden brown and cooked through.

10. Let cool slightly on a wire rack before serving with clotted cream and strawberry jam.

60) Mini Lemon Tarts:

- Mini tart shells (store-bought or homemade)
- Lemon curd (store-bought or homemade)
- Fresh berries (such as raspberries or blueberries), for garnish
- Powdered sugar, for dusting

Instructions:

1. If using store-bought mini tart shells, follow package instructions for baking and let cool completely.
2. Spoon lemon curd into cooled tart shells, filling each shell almost to the top.
3. Arrange fresh berries on top of the lemon curd.
4. Dust with powdered sugar just before serving.

Tea Selection

Offer a variety of teas such as:

- Earl Grey
- English Breakfast

- Green tea

- Herbal teas like chamomile or peppermint

Presentation Tips

- **Tiered Cake Stands:** Arrange sandwiches and sweets on tiered cake stands for an elegant presentation.

- **Tea Accessories:** Provide sugar cubes, lemon wedges, and milk or cream for tea drinkers to customize their beverages.

- **Decorative Touches:** Garnish plates with fresh herbs, edible flowers, or lemon twists for a visually appealing spread.

Serving

Serve your afternoon tea spread on a beautifully set table with fine china and linen napkins. Encourage guests to relax and enjoy the selection of savory sandwiches, classic scones with clotted cream and jam, mini lemon tarts, and a variety of teas. This traditional British-style tea service is perfect for any afternoon gathering or special occasion.

APPENDICES

GOLOSARY OF TERMS

1. **Al dente**: Italian term meaning "to the tooth," used to describe pasta that is cooked firm to the bite.

2. **Braise**: A cooking method where food (usually meat) is first browned and then cooked slowly in a covered pot with a small amount of liquid.

3. **Broil**: To cook food directly under a heat source, usually in an oven.

4. **Caramelize**: To heat sugar until it liquefies and becomes a caramel color.

5. **Chiffonade**: A cutting technique where leafy greens or herbs are rolled tightly and sliced into thin ribbons.

6. **Deglaze**: To add liquid (such as broth) to a pan to dissolve and incorporate the browned bits left after sautéing or roasting.

7. **Dredge**: To coat food with flour, breadcrumbs, or cornmeal before cooking.

8. **Emulsion**: A mixture of two liquids that usually don't combine smoothly, like oil and vinegar in salad dressing.

9. **Fillet**: To remove bones from meat or fish, or to cut into boneless pieces.

10. **Fold**: To gently combine ingredients by using a cutting motion with a spoon or spatula, typically used in baking.

11. **Julienne**: A cutting technique where food is cut into thin matchstick-shaped strips.

12. **Marinate**: To soak food in a seasoned liquid to enhance flavor or tenderize before cooking.

13. **Parchment paper**: A kitchen paper used to line baking pans or for wrapping food for cooking.

14. **Poach**: To cook food gently in simmering liquid, usually water or broth.

15. **Roux**: A mixture of flour and fat (usually butter) used to thicken sauces or soups.

16. **Sear**: To brown the surface of meat quickly over high heat to seal in juices.

17. **Simmer**: To cook food gently in liquid just below the boiling point.

18. **Steam**: To cook food by exposing it to steam from boiling water.

19. **Zest**: The outer, colored part of citrus fruit peel, used to add flavor to dishes.

20. **Halal**: Food and practices that are permissible under Islamic law.

21. **Brining**: Soaking food in a saltwater solution to enhance flavor and moisture retention.

22. **Compote**: Fruit stewed or cooked in syrup.

23. **Confit**: A method of cooking meat slowly in its own fat or oil.

24. **Crème brûlée**: A dessert consisting of rich custard topped with a layer of hardened caramelized sugar.

25. **Dashi**: A Japanese cooking stock made from Kombu (seaweed) and bonito flakes.

26. **Fermentation**: The process of breaking down sugars into alcohol or organic acids using microorganisms like yeast or bacteria.

27. **Fricassee**: A cooking method where meat is first sautéed and then stewed in liquid.

28. **Ganache**: A mixture of chocolate and cream used as a filling or frosting.

29. **Jus**: French term for natural juices released from cooking meat.

30. **Macerate**: To soften food by soaking it in liquid, often with sugar or alcohol.

31. **Meunière**: A cooking method where fish is dredged in flour and sautéed, typically served with browned butter and lemon.

32. **Mirepoix**: A mixture of diced vegetables (onion, carrot, celery) used as a flavor base for sauces, soups, and stews.

33. **Parboil**: To partially cook food in boiling water or steam before finishing by another method.

34. **Pâté**: A smooth paste of seasoned ground meat or liver.

35. **Reduction**: The process of thickening and intensifying flavors in a liquid by boiling.

36. **Roulade**: A dish made by rolling ingredients like meat or pastry around a filling.

37. **Sauté**: To cook food quickly in a small amount of oil or butter over high heat.

38. **Scald**: To heat a liquid, usually milk, to just below boiling.

39. **Sous vide**: A cooking technique where food is vacuum-sealed in a bag and cooked at a precise temperature in a water bath.

40. **Tartare**: Finely chopped raw meat or fish mixed with seasonings and served as an appetizer.

41. **Velouté**: A sauce made from stock and a roux, often used as a base for other sauces.

42. **Wok**: A versatile round-bottomed cooking vessel used in Chinese cuisine for stir-frying, steaming, and deep-frying.

43. **Yield**: The amount of food or cooked product obtained from a given recipe or quantity of ingredients.

44. **Zester**: A kitchen tool used to remove zest from citrus fruits.

45. **Au gratin**: Topped with breadcrumbs or cheese and browned in the oven or under a broiler.

46. **Bain-marie**: A water bath used to cook delicate dishes like custards and cheesecakes evenly.

47. **Blanch**: To briefly cook food in boiling water, then plunge into ice water to stop cooking.

48. **Chop**: To cut food into small, irregular pieces.

49. **Degrease**: To remove fat from the surface of liquid, usually by skimming or using a fat separator.

50. **En papillote**: A cooking method where food is enclosed in parchment paper or foil and baked.

51. **Flambé**: To ignite alcohol (such as brandy or rum) to burn off the alcohol and flavor a dish.

52. **Garnish**: Edible decorations or enhancements added to a dish before serving.

53. **Infuse**: To steep ingredients (such as herbs or tea leaves) in liquid to extract flavor.

54. **Knead**: To work dough with hands to develop gluten and create elasticity.

55. **Ladle**: A large spoon with a deep bowl used for serving soups and stews.

56. **Mince**: To finely chop food into tiny, uniform pieces.

57. **Pâtissier**: A pastry chef specializing in desserts and pastries.

58. **Red-eye gravy**: A Southern American gravy made from pan drippings and coffee.

59. **Sear**: To quickly brown the surface of meat at high heat to lock in juices.

60. **Spatchcock**: To remove the backbone of poultry and flatten before cooking.

61. **Supreme**: To remove the segments of citrus fruit from the membrane.

62. **Truss**: To tie poultry or meat with kitchen twine to hold its shape during cooking.

63. **Vinaigrette**: A dressing made from oil, vinegar, and seasonings.

64. **Wilt**: To cook leafy greens briefly until they become limp.

65. **Yolk**: The yellow part of an egg, rich in fat and nutrients.

66. **Zest**: The outermost part of citrus fruit peel, used to add flavor to dishes.

67. **Aioli**: A Mediterranean sauce made from garlic, olive oil, and egg yolks.

68. **Baste**: To spoon or brush liquids (such as melted butter or pan drippings) over food while cooking.

69. **Caponata**: Sicilian dish of eggplant, celery, tomatoes, olives, and capers cooked in sweet and sour sauce.

70. **Dollop**: A small portion of soft food, such as whipped cream or mashed potatoes, dropped onto another food item.

71. **Escabeche**: A Spanish dish of marinated fish or meat, typically served cold as an appetizer.

72. **Fumet**: A concentrated fish stock used as a base for sauces and soups.

73. **Ghee**: Clarified butter used in Indian cooking.

74. **Hors d'oeuvre**: Small savory dishes served as appetizers before a meal.

75. **Kosher**: Food prepared according to Jewish dietary laws.

76. **Legumes**: Plants that produce edible seeds, such as beans and lentils.

77. **Marmalade**: A preserve made from citrus fruits, typically bitter oranges.

78. **Nutmeg**: A spice made from the seed of the nutmeg tree, used in both sweet and savory dishes.

79. **Oyster sauce**: A thick, dark brown sauce made from oysters and soy sauce, used in Asian cooking.

80. **Pâté de foie gras**: A rich paste made from the liver of a duck or goose.

81. **Quiche**: A savory open pastry crust filled with eggs, cream, and various ingredients such as cheese, vegetables, or meat.

82. **Ramekin**: A small dish used for baking individual portions of food.

83. **Sashimi**: Thinly sliced raw fish or seafood, often served with soy sauce and wasabi.

84. **Tamarind**: A tangy fruit pod used in cooking and as a flavoring for sauces and drinks.

85. **Umami**: The fifth taste, often described as savory or meaty.

86. **Vermicelli**: Thin pasta resembling spaghetti but finer.

87. **Wonton**: Chinese dumpling filled with minced meat or vegetables, typically served in soup.

88. **Xanthan gum**: A thickening agent used in food production, especially gluten-free baking.

89. **Yuzu**: A citrus fruit native to East Asia, prized for its aromatic zest and juice.

90. **Za'atar**: A Middle Eastern spice blend of herbs, sesame seeds, and sumac.

91. **Ampalaya**: Bitter gourd or bitter melon, used in Asian cuisines for its distinct bitter flavor.

92. **Chermoula**: A North African marinade and sauce made from herbs, spices, and oil, used on fish, meats, and vegetables.

93. **Dukkah**: An Egyptian spice mix of nuts, seeds, and spices, often used as a dip with bread and olive oil.

94. **Einkorn**: An ancient variety of wheat with a nutty flavor, used in baking and cooking.

95. **Fregola**: Sardinian pasta similar to couscous, made from semolina dough that is rolled into small balls and toasted.

96. **Garam masala**: A blend of ground spices used extensively in Indian cuisine, often added towards the end of cooking.

97. **Harissa**: A North African chili paste made from roasted red peppers, spices, and herbs, used as a condiment or marinade.

98. **Icing sugar**: Finely powdered sugar used for frosting and decorating cakes and pastries.

These terms cover a wide range of cooking techniques, ingredients, and culinary practices that will be useful for your readers as they explore the world of cooking and baking in your book.

REFERENCES

Certainly! Here are some additional reading materials and references that you can consider including in your book:

1. **Books:**

    - McGee, Harold. *On Food and Cooking: The Science and Lore of the Kitchen.* Scribner, 2004.

    - Ruhlman, Michael. *Ratio: The Simple Codes behind the Craft of Everyday Cooking.* Scribner, 2009.

    - Child, Julia, et al. *Mastering the Art of French Cooking.* Knopf, 1961.

    - Pollan, Michael. *The Omnivore's Dilemma: A Natural History of Four Meals.* Penguin Books, 2006.

2. **Websites:**

    - Serious Eats (seriouseats.com): Provides in-depth articles on cooking techniques, recipes, and food science.

    - The Kitchn (thekitchn.com): Offers recipes, cooking tips, and kitchen organization advice.

- America's Test Kitchen (americastestkitchen.com): Known for scientifically testing recipes and cooking equipment.

3. **Scientific Journals and Articles:**

    - Journal of Food Science
    - Food Chemistry
    - Journal of Agricultural and Food Chemistry

4. **Online Courses and Educational Platforms:**

    - Coursera (coursera.org): Offers courses on culinary arts, food science, and nutrition.
    - EdX (edx.org): Provides courses from universities and institutions on cooking techniques and food chemistry.

5. **Documentaries and Films:**

    - *Chef's Table* (Netflix series): Profiles renowned chefs and explores their culinary philosophies.
    - *Jiro Dreams of Sushi* (2011): A documentary film about sushi chef Jiro Ono and his dedication to his craft.

- *Salt Fat Acid Heat* (Netflix series): Explores the fundamental elements of cooking through the lens of these four essentials.

Including references like these will enrich your book with additional resources for readers who want to delve deeper into the science, techniques, and cultural aspects of cooking and food preparation.